Praise for *Kirkpatrick's Investment and Trading Strategies*

"Charles Kirkpatrick has been producing top-notch work for years, as evidenced by his multiple Dow Awards and top-rated books. And his work keeps getting better. He doesn't just hypothesize about market movements. He backs up his ideas with real, quantified data. This book is another very impressive addition to the Charles Kirkpatrick library of work. Well done!"

—**Rob Hanna,** founder of QuantifiableEdges.com and OvernightEdges.com

"Kirkpatrick's latest work is a great companion to his book *Beat the Market: Invest by Knowing What Stocks to Buy and What Stocks to Sell.* He walks the reader step by step through his logic and then demonstrates the results by statistically valid test procedures. This is the Kirkpatrick Investment Theory updated and proven, plus a few extra studies to improve performance once again.

"For those of us who use his approach regularly, his latest work will improve and confirm his investment concepts. For those not familiar with his work, this book may inspire them to rethink what methods they are using. The backtested results are that impressive.

"Kirkpatrick's latest work addresses two significant areas. First, his investment approach is reviewed, tested, and refinements applied; then it is retested using walk forward techniques. The other area covered, and one that should not be overlooked, is his testing techniques and theories on how to evaluate stock selection and portfolio changes. He shows the reader how to focus on significant parameters that are most important while trying to avoid the dangers of optimization. The result is a robust system with a high probability of excellent performance in the future."

—**Thomas Hamilton,** President of Special Risk Capital Management, LLC

"When someone has been successfully involved in the markets and in particular technical analysis for almost half a century, you should pay attention to what he has to say. Charlie Kirkpatrick is such a person, one who has a solid grasp of how markets work and how to develop a process for profiting in them. I cannot begin to count the number of times I have read about someone's system and found that it was poorly designed, inadequately tested, and in many cases, used for some other motive than to provide a systematic approach to profiting in the market. Charlie has conquered all of these shortcomings in this book with a solid, well-constructed, thoroughly documented, and viable approach to systematic trading."

—**Gregory L. Morris,** author of *Dancing with the Trend*, Chairman of Investment Committee, and Chief Technical Analyst of Stadion Money Management, LLC

"On the Venn diagram of financial market study, this book fits into the coveted overlap between technical, quantitative, and fundamental approaches. It addresses one of the key questions that all three methods ask: How can the relative performance of stocks to one another be used to create a profitable investing approach? Kirkpatrick walks the reader through the necessary elements to comprehend and build robust market timing and stock selection systems. He addresses the murky issues of optimization and quantifying trend and also focuses in on his preferred indicators and uses for cycle analysis, based on 40+ years of market experience. No fancy software required—Kirkpatrick presents systems that can be implemented and managed using the most basic of tools. A great read for anyone looking to approach the markets more systematically, making the most of their capital and time."

Hima Reddy, CMT, author of *The Trading Methodologies of W.D. Gann*

Kirkpatrick's Investment and Trading Strategies

Tools and Techniques for Profitable Trend Following

Charles D. Kirkpatrick II, CMT

Vice President, Publisher: Tim Moore
Associate Publisher and Director of Marketing: Amy Neidlinger
Executive Editor: Jim Boyd
Operations Specialist: Jodi Kemper
Marketing Manager: Lisa Loftus
Cover Designer: Chuti Prasertsith
Managing Editor: Kristy Hart
Senior Project Editor: Betsy Gratner
Copy Editor: Karen Annett
Proofreader: Williams Woods Publishing Services
Indexer: Lisa Stumpf
Compositor: Nonie Ratcliff
Manufacturing Buyer: Dan Uhrig

© 2014 by Charles D. Kirkpatrick II
Published by Pearson Education, Inc.
Publishing as FT Press
Upper Saddle River, New Jersey 07458

FT Press offers excellent discounts on this book when ordered in quantity for bulk purchases
or special sales. For more information, please contact U.S. Corporate and Government Sales,
1-800-382-3419, corpsales@pearsontechgroup.com. For sales outside the U.S., please contact
International Sales at international@pearsoned.com.

Printed in the United States of America

First Printing: July 2013

ISBN-10: 0-13-259661-X
ISBN-13: 978-0-13-259661-9

Pearson Education LTD.
Pearson Education Australia PTY, Limited.
Pearson Education Singapore, Pte. Ltd.
Pearson Education Asia, Ltd.
Pearson Education Canada, Ltd.
Pearson Educación de Mexico, S.A. de C.V.
Pearson Education—Japan
Pearson Education Malaysia, Pte. Ltd.

Library of Congress Control Number: 2013939858

To James C. Boyd,
who was with me in the beginning.

Contents

Acknowledgments

I cannot enumerate all the wonderful people through my 47+ years of technical analysis who have helped me in many large and small ways. I can only thank all of you for your ease of access and willingness to share ideas, studies, methods, and references.

I wish to also thank the people at Pearson Education and FT Press for their patience and ability in producing this tome: Russ Hall, Amy Neidlinger, Kristy Hart, Betsy Gratner, and Karen Annett. I do miss my old editor, Jim Boyd, who stuck with me for better or worse through three different publications and retired this year.

For this specific book, I am indebted to the folks at tradingblox.com: Amin, Karl, Sandra, and especially Jake Carriker, who did much of the walk-forward and indexing programming for the stock selection section.

My initial advice on how to attack the walk-forward optimization on my meager PC was bolstered by the critical knowledge and assistance from old friends at the Research Computing and Instrumentation Center of the University of New Hampshire: Bill Lenharth, Bob Anderson, and Patrick Messer.

To integrate stock market data with all its quirks and errors, Commodity Systems, Inc., was most helpful, especially Nassrin Berns, Rudolph Cabral, and the elusive Debbie and Sierra.

And for editing my hashed English, I am indebted to my coauthor of our earlier technical analysis textbook, Julie Dahquist, and my future daughter-in-law, Zoe Litsios.

And as always, I could never have completed this book without the kindness, forbearance, and support of my lifetime partner and love, Ellie, who for more than 51 years has been by my side.

Kittery, Maine
May 19, 2013

About the Author

Charles D. Kirkpatrick II, CMT, has spent 47+ years in investing as a security analyst, portfolio manager, block desk trader, options trader, and institutional broker. He is President of Kirkpatrick & Company, Inc., a technical analysis research firm that publishes the *Market Strategist* investment newsletter. He has appeared on CNBC and *Wall Street Week* and has been quoted in *Barron's, Money,* and *BusinessWeek*. A past instructor in finance at the School of Business Administration, Fort Lewis College, and Adjunct Professor of Finance at Brandeis University International Business School, he is a two-time winner of the Market Technicians Association's prestigious Charles H. Dow Award for research in technical analysis, winner of the MTA Annual Award in 2008 for "outstanding contributions to the field of technical analysis," and winner in 2012 of the Mike Epstein Award from the MTA Educational Foundation for "long-term sponsorship of Technical Analysis in Academia." He is a Chartered Market Technician, a past member of the board of directors of the Market Technicians Association, past Editor of the *Journal of Technical Analysis*, past board member and Vice-President of the Market Technicians Association Educational Foundation, and a member of the American Association of Professional Technicians (AAPTA). He coauthored *Technical Analysis: The Complete Source for Financial Market Technicians*, the primary textbook for the CMT program and for university graduate courses on technical analysis, authored *Beat the Market* and, most recently, *Time the Markets: Using Technical Analysis to Interpret Economic Data*. He is a graduate of Phillips Exeter Academy, Harvard College (AB), and the Wharton School (MBA) and lives with his wife in Maine.

www.charleskirkpatrick.com

Preface

I find I am most challenged by the ocean and the trading markets. I respect them because they are both such a challenge to outwit. Both have similarities. The ocean can be beautiful, but it also can be deadly. Same with the market: It can be deadly or calm. The other similar aspect is that neither gives a damn about me or anyone else. They are individual forces that have strength beyond our mortal powers. Often they are personalized, as "mother nature" or "Mr. Market," but they are not personal. They are physically apparent but operate with complete indifference to us and others. Indeed, the challenge in interacting with them is that of learning when they are friendly and when they are not. We make our profits in friendly markets, and we sail comfortably and safely when the ocean is friendly. The most important point about both is that we can try to understand when circumstances are favorable for us, but we will never understand the entire picture of the oceans or the markets. So our endeavor is to discover how to anticipate the friendliness of both, when to invest and when not, and when to sail and when not. We make mistakes because the markets and oceans can rapidly change character, or we make mistakes because our analysis is wrong. It is a frustrating exercise but one filled with thrills, joy, sadness, fear, greed, and sometimes accomplishment. These are our personal emotions, not those of the indifferent markets or ocean. Thus, we tend to make many mistakes by being emotional in an unsympathetic world. We learn that to take advantage of the friendly times, we must be equally as unsympathetic, be critical of our decisions and our mistakes, not blame the inanimate world for our inadequacies, and must utilize only those strategies that come from pure, unemotional reason.

1

Introduction

I write this book to describe and test the concepts I use in my favorite investment and trading strategies. These concepts are not new by themselves but are newly applied to these strategies and should become the basis for the honest study of all stock-picking methods. I use the walk-forward method of optimizing all strategies as this is to me the best and most realistic means of testing and analyzing an algorithmic system. More about the specifics of these concepts and how they work follows in the succeeding chapters as I progress through the particulars of these systems. I explain what I believe to be the only way that the uninformed, disconnected, otherwise busy, time-limited, poorly financed, stock market outsider can still compete with the "big boys."

Discretionary Versus Algorithmic Trading or Investing

Discretionary investing occurs when all decisions are made by the investor. Success is rare and depends on knowledge, expertise, quick decision making, and the ability to master emotions, biases, and mood. Most people lose money in investing because they act on rumor, advice, intuition, hunch, incorrect information, poor judgment, or any number of other inputs into their investment decisions. There are very successful discretionary investors, such as Warren Buffett, George Soros, Paul Tudor Jones, and T. Boone Pickens. You and I are not in this class. We need help and discipline as well as the ability to determine when to buy and sell. The psyche of these billionaires is hard-wired to select and to time investments. Most people are lacking in this ability; that is why they consistently lose money and are forced out of the markets with losses. Even many so-called professionals are unable to invest successfully. The poor performance of most professionally run mutual funds and pension funds demonstrates this universal shortcoming. So how do you and I survive in the trading markets when we don't have intrinsic discretionary investment ability?

The answer has been around for many years but only recently available in an easily applicable form. Robert Pardo (2008)[1] argues, and I tend to agree, that two events have occurred in markets in the past 20 years that can help the outsider. One is the expansion of markets to include financial derivatives. Financial derivatives, those financial instruments that derive their value from another security, provide hedging and speculation in large, liquid markets that only recently have become available to the average investor. Second, Pardo argues, is the availability of cheap, fast computing power. None of the data testing done in this book would have been available to you or me 20 years ago. The ability to rapidly calculate large amounts of data has made it possible to test theories of investment that had long been simply passed down from trader to trader, investor to investor. I add a third event to the list: the ability to execute a buy or sell order inexpensively, efficiently, and rapidly. Electronic exchanges have changed the entire investment field: The old, stodgy investment manager calling his broker to execute an order is an event of the distant past.

These character changes in the markets and speedier ancillary facilities have made it possible to develop investment systems that can be proven statistically and operated almost mechanically. These systems are called *algorithmic systems* because they are nondiscretionary and operate solely on an algorithm or series of algorithms invented for the specific purpose of profiting in the marketplace. By using proven mechanical strategies that don't require the expertise and knowledge of successful discretionary investors, algorithms circumvent the intrinsic human inability to profit in the markets.

However, algorithmic trading requires strict sets of well-defined rules. Even when a system is tested and perfected, the investor can still become discouraged, bored, unhappy with the immediate results, or bothered by drawdowns to such a point that he will abandon the successful system and thus lose whatever advantage he had derived from it. This is human nature, a nature not compatible with trading markets. Therefore, even though an algorithmic system can be developed, optimized, and tested in multiple ways, the user still has the impulse to abandon it. So, to be successful in algorithmic systems, not only must the investor or trader spend time and mental power to develop and test the system, but he must also have the willpower, discipline, and patience not to waver from it.

This book demonstrates and explains algorithmic systems for both investment and for trading. It uses specific rules to enter and exit individual stocks. These rules are derived from statistical methods of optimization that give a better-than-even chance of success, a definite edge, in the marketplace. No system is perfect or without losses, of course, but these limitations are understood and have been taken into consideration and study. The final algorithms in this book are as accurate and profitable as possible under present methods of backtesting. Ask yourself if your personal method has produced the same performance results as these systems. If it has, then you are in the same exalted league as the masters I mentioned previously, and you can throw this book away.

Why This Book?

I write this book because I am disheartened by the general lack of investment common sense and because it hurts me that so much money has been lost when it could easily have been kept. As one who has practiced on Wall Street for more than 47 years, has taught technical analysis at the graduate-school level, and has been awarded many honors by my peers, I describe in this book, point-by-point, the best investment methods for profitable investing and trading stock trends I have found over a lifetime of professional study. People often ask me about the stock market, with questions such as the following:

- "I have lost a lot of money in the stock market. Should I quit and just buy mutual funds, ETFs, or government bonds?"
- "What should I do?"
- "How do I compete with the professionals in selecting stocks?"
- "How do I know when it is time to sell?"

This book examines in detail an investment system of stock selection for investors and several indicators as well as a system for traders. As in any serious pursuit, it takes some work by the participant, but once the system is set up, the work should take an hour each week at most. It may require a subscription to a data service or charting service, though many are now free on the Internet. I also include several trading systems that are short-term and use hourly price data. They require more work, more information, more time, better execution of trades, and the ability to sell short.

The meat of this book is described in easily understood terms for anyone familiar with the technical aspects of the stock market. Not one to just describe what to do, I test with modern statistical tests to show the best combination of indicators to use. The results of these tests fully demonstrate how you can successfully apply them.

Recent times in the stock market have been difficult for amateur and professional alike. Investors have been burned in the stock market and are distrustful of "methods" or "systems." They are also skeptical of new books on investment methods, suspecting that those methods are suppositions or unsubstantiated promises by the author to sell books or an advisory service. This book is different, as are my previous books, because I actually test the methods I describe. Very few books do this, and those that do often suffer from flawed techniques. I test methods because I want readers to understand that these work. This book is not, however, a treatise on the follies of conventional investment analysis. Instead, it is a book that describes the logic and particulars of how to invest and trade successfully in stocks using statistically demonstrated systems.

I often use the term *system*. As a term, it may have negative connotations in other endeavors, but in the context of investing and trading, a system is a set of rules for buying and selling that is uninhibited by discretionary decisions and has been backtested for verity and robustness (that is, stability). Usually, systems are technical, in that they only utilize prices and configurations of trading statistics, but not always. Many successful systems use fundamental, economic data, or a combination of both fundamental and technical. The O'Neil CANSLIM method, for example, is a combined system as is the value line method of ranking stocks. When a system is purely technical, however, it may turn off people who don't believe in technical analysis.

During the time I worked as an institutional salesman, I met many institutional investment managers who did not trust technical analysis. Because of this, they mistrusted the relative strength method I was selling, continuing to do so even after I had demonstrated its success in real time with their own portfolio and investment lists. The managers seemed to reject technical analysis based on advice they had heard from contemporary managers and courses they had taken at their business schools. It was at that time I decided to focus on teaching and introducing technical analysis to business school curricula where most of these portfolio managers had gained their misinformation and bias against technical analysis. This book uses a few technical indicators, those that I have found to be excellent when used properly. I describe them and their use in detail, as well as test their validity in selecting and discarding stocks.

Investing Is a Business

People tend to treat investment as a specialty having to do with picking the right investments and selling them when they become successful. However, investment is a business, just like a hardware store, where items are bought with the intention of selling them at higher prices than what was paid for them and liquidating those items that don't sell well. It is an inventory management business where losers are eliminated and winners are accumulated. Unfortunately, the investment management business doesn't quite look at investments this way. For one, portfolio managers and investors are reticent to sell investments at a loss. There is a documented and well-studied psychological fear of admitting failure in the markets. But does the hardware store manager castigate himself for dumping goods that don't sell? Perhaps a little, but the successful manager dumps them in a sale, hopes to break even, and expands the products that are profitable. In other words, the manager's ego, while dented slightly, doesn't interfere with the successful business of selling hardware goods. On the other hand, ego tends to run portfolios, rather than common sense. Not surprisingly, the hardware business and the markets don't care about ego. The market is neutral, dispassionate, nonjudgmental, and as some egotists anthropomorphize, "cruel." But to profit in the market, just as in a retail business, ego must be subordinate to reality. Reality is that the business or portfolio manager is not perfect nor is his decision making. The decision-making process depends on too many variables and facts that can be inaccurate, irrelevant, or that can change. It also depends on experience, knowledge, and discipline. Errors in judgment are common and must be rectified immediately, especially in trading. The law of percentages (50% loss requires a 100% gain to break even) is against the indecisive manager when an initial decision is incorrect.

Strategies

Investment management consists of three basic strategies. Two have to do with the management of activity, buying and selling. The third is a strategy not covered in this book: how to manage portfolio risk called *money management.* In individual investments, a stock must be picked and then bought, the bought stocks must be sold at some time, and the whole process must be managed for risk. The first is called *entry strategy;* the second is called *exit strategy.* Exit strategy is also called *risk management.* The third strategy is *money management* or *portfolio management.* No investment program can succeed without all three. Unfortunately, most portfolio managers and investors focus on entry, and relegate exit and money management to the bottom of their priorities. Ironically, the reason most professional managers and investors consistently lose money is that the latter two are the more important.

In my graduate-school classes on technical analysis, I ask students to randomly pick a stock, regardless of its earnings, management, industry, and so forth and rather than analyze those particulars, invest on the flip of a coin. Using the price history of their chosen stock over the previous six months, they are to record the results of each transaction. At a coin flip of heads, the entry signal is to buy, and at a flip of tails to sell short. This is their entry strategy. Using an equal dollar amount of shares for each transaction so as not to be influenced by position size, they are to record holding the position until they exit their position on the exit rules. They are to close the position when either it has a 5% loss or it has retraced from its most profitable gain by 5%. In other words, if the student buys a stock at 100, he then either sells it at 95 (5% loss) or at a retracement of 5% from its most profitable price. Say the stock runs to 130 and then retraces 5% to 123.50. The position is then closed for a gain of 23.5%. In a short sale, the procedure is the same only the risk is 5% above the short-sale price. This is their exit strategy. On the day after a position is closed, they are to start the process over again by flipping a coin and acting according to the original instructions.

Of course, in this simple system, it helps to have a volatile stock. Dull stock behavior won't produce many transactions and thus little profit. This, in itself, is a lesson on why volatility is a desirable facet of investment and especially trading, provided risk of loss is controlled, as it is in this experiment. Do all of the students make money? No, but a plurality do, enough so that if a portfolio were constructed of all the students' individual experiments, it would consistently make money. The lesson: Buying or short-selling a stock is not the most important aspect of investment—it was done on the flip of a coin. Selling and controlling risk are the most important and why an explicit exit strategy is necessary.

Entry Strategy

There are many excellent entry strategies, both fundamental and technical. Several recent books have described fundamental strategies using various corporate statistics and have given statistical evidence on their merits. The problem of selecting stocks has been well researched and is available in book form for anyone to learn.

In my earlier investment book, *Beat the Market*,[2] I demonstrated methods I found at the time to be the best for selecting stocks and for timing their purchase and sale. This system included a screening of all U.S. stocks for those that had the best recent history of price rise, called *relative strength*. I also used two screens of fundamental, company-specific information. These were relative earnings growth and relative price-to-sales. The 2006 study included figures going back to 1998. It was an evaluation of a system that had been operating live for nine years, but it was not an optimization for the best parameters. I only looked at what had happened with predetermined parameters from the 1970s.

Until relatively recently, to prove the validity of a systematic method, analysts had to develop a hypothesis, perhaps backtest it, and calculate it each day and measure the results on paper for a long period to see if it actually worked. The process was similar to the scientific method of hypothesis, trial, and confirmation or rejection. Because my earlier study used weekly data only, the time necessary for conclusive results was long, often many years. I am getting older now and don't have the time ahead to do such tests again. Thankfully, the computer, easily accessible stock market price data, and new methods of backtesting have been developed and are being used by students of the markets today to investigate systems without waiting years for results.

The primary testing method I now use is called *walk-forward optimizing*. It optimizes segments of price data in the past; for each segment, it finds the best fit for a proposed system and tests it in data that is not part of the optimization. It duplicates as well as possible the earlier lengthy method of waiting for results. When properly constructed, it covers substantial periods of time in deriving the optimizations to represent all kinds of markets over time; it runs through a number of different sequences to ensure the results are not a "best fit" to existing data; and it uses a substantial amount of data, enough to include real-time anomalies in the tests. When it fails to show a robust system, the failure is useful because it shuts off further inquiry in the direction of that failure and often suggests other approaches that may be better. Once this optimization is completed and the results show a viable system is present, the probability of it working in the future is high. Of course, there is no guarantee that the system will prove to be viable in the future, but the odds are significantly increased by the use of out-of-sample testing within the optimization.

I know from past history, professional and academic literature, and from watching its success in live markets that there is validity to the relative price strength method, but when I began, I did not know the specific parameters that would be optimal. Earlier parameters had been somewhat arbitrarily derived years before the long-term test began. For example, Bob Levy, who originated the method in the late 1960s, suggested a lookback period for the calculation of relative strength of 26 weeks. He had tried periods of 4 weeks through 52 weeks, finding that 52 weeks worked but not as well as 26 weeks and that 4 weeks gave a negative performance. Thus, I used 26 weeks in the original formula and followed its use for more than 30 years. You will see later in this book, when I get to the actual tests of relative strength, that the optimal lookback is similar to what was hypothesized. I test not only the lookback period but also the ideal buy rank and sell rank, the minimum volume and price necessary to profit, and the percent protective stop. I assume that most investors and portfolio managers using relative strength as a stock selection method are interested only in taking investment positions. The emphasis in this book in the investment section is thus on holding long positions only. Short-selling is presented in the second section of this book on trading strategies beginning in Chapter 6, "Trading Strategies."

My earlier method of stock selection worked in historical testing for a few years. The relative earnings growth never worked, and the relative price-to-sales ratio never came close as a separate selection criteria to the success from relative price strength alone, but it did prove useful at market peaks. Since then, I've found that a relative price-to-sales screen is not fruitful, detracting from the performance of relatively strong stocks. I also found that the relative strength itself was not providing the spectacular results it had in the past. I knew from having watched these figures in real time for more than 30 years that there were periods when they didn't work, but I had to admit that I never investigated the best all-round parameters. I notice in O'Shaughnessy's fourth edition of his book *What Works on Wall*

Street (2012)[3] that he also has found that price-to-sales is no longer a highly rated selection means, yet he still maintains that relative price strength is the best selection method of all, though his calculation and lookback are quite different from mine. So I have eliminated price-to-sales and continue with just relative price strength, back to my roots as a technical analyst, a place where I feel more comfortable.

Limiting Capital Loss—Drawdown, Volatility, and Diversification

Most investment managers and portfolio managers don't have an explicit exit strategy and thus have no idea of what their potential capital risk may be. The next time you sit down with your investment manager or read literature on your mutual fund, look for evidence of an explicit exit strategy. You'll be surprised how vague is their coverage, if at all, of closing positions and limiting capital risk. As demonstrated in the student experiment, it is the limiting of the losses that provides the profit, not the stock picking. This is the same principle that the hardware store owner faces: Limit loss and hold profit.

There are many ways to limit loss, most of them technical, having to do with the price action of the security itself. It is very difficult to have an exit strategy based on earnings, sales, or any of the scores of fundamental factors that accompany a stock. O'Shaughnessy has experimented with fundamental factors that consistently cause losses or underperformance, but even his study avoids the question of when to sell a stock either to protect against loss or to protect against loss of accumulated gain. So technical analysis, the study of price action, is the primary method of protecting against loss and even more importantly is the primary method of determining risk of loss.

Drawdown, the amount by which a portfolio can decline from its highest value to its lowest value, is the best measure of risk. It quantifies the percentage and dollars at risk. Drawdown is the ultimate risk of capital. A 100% drawdown means you have been wiped out.

A lesser drawdown may be impossible for you to mentally and emotionally withstand. You should understand what you will accept as the largest loss and approach your investments with that in mind. Most investors are willing to accept a loss of as much as 20% in a drawdown, provided the upside performance potential is two to three times better. The relationship between acceptable gains versus drawdown is personal. Some commodity speculators are willing to take 60% to 80% drawdowns, but they know their system will eventually double or triple their investment. It is a standard rule that gains and drawdowns are related and that you cannot have substantial gains without being able to accept sizable drawdowns.

Volatility is a measure of how much a price oscillates back and forth. It is never a constant, as volatility changes with market conditions and the stock's trend. It also doesn't tell you what your dollar or percentage capital risk might be. Volatility should never be the primary gauge of risk. Whereas drawdown is forever, volatility as a risk measure is limited. No volatility value can tell you that you will be wiped out. Unbelievably, recent academic and professional literature focuses on volatility as something to avoid. Yet, volatility is where profits are made and is thus something to seek. Loss comes from drawdown, not volatility. In my student exercise, it was the curtailing of loss through the 5% protective exit, limiting my drawdown to 5%, that allowed the upward volatility to profit. The drawdown was controlled with the 5% limit. Measures like the Sharpe ratio, a common measure of risk, that contain a divisor based on volatility are deceiving because they include both up and down volatility. An investment should always have a large upward volatility—you can't profit from a dull stock—and have a limit on its downside volatility.

Sharpe ratio figures are incorrectly presented as measures of risk. Because of the universality of this misconception, portfolio managers in most firms have to include their Sharpe ratio in reports of their performance to show risk. This convention is also seen in most mutual fund monitoring services and most literature from mutual fund companies. This public display of volatility as a measure of risk forces portfolio managers, who must compete in the performance world, to buy stocks with lower-than-average volatility so as to keep their risk low. They thus are forced to buy stocks that are not trending, yet what is necessary for substantial profit with limited capital risk is a strong, steeply rising, volatile stock price, a price-related method of selling to protect against initial loss in case the investment turns out to be a poor one, and a price-related method of selling to avoid losing a majority of the gain from a successful one.

Volatility calculated as the standard deviation of prices is also a false volatility yet it is included in the Black-Scholes option pricing model. When a security is in an upward trend, where the price is rapidly advancing, standard deviation includes the strength of the trend as well as variability around it. In other words, a rising stock will have a high standard deviation because by being in a trend, the price deviates significantly from its mean. If such a calculation of volatility is used as a measure of risk, it thus excludes a strong stock from investment consideration because a strong stock is by this definition very risky. This is nonsense. The many professional and academic studies of the relative strength concept prove that price strength is profitable. Indeed, upside volatility is desirable, not something to fear. It is the risk of capital loss, something totally different, that is worrisome. I don't know if the prejudice about technical analysis is the cause of this misapplication of volatility as a concept or not, but it is unrealistic and has led to many portfolio disasters.

Another misconception is that *diversification* is the solution to avoid poor stock selection. It assumes that the investment decision will be wrong sometimes, but that if enough stocks are owned, the total loss will be dampened by the success of the profitable stocks. This philosophy is a misplaced result of the Capital Asset Pricing Model principally because it relies on what is called "beta" as a risk measure. Beta is a measure of how closely a stock's price changes mimic the changes in a market average such as the Standard & Poor's

500. When the linear relationship between a stock price change and a market average change is plotted on a graph, the point at which the line crosses the vertical axis is called the alpha, and the slope of the line is called the beta. A steep slope, and thus a high beta, is considered to be a sign of high volatility. However, while being represented as a measure of risk, it tells nothing about the chances of capital loss in the stock. All beta does is measure the oscillations of the stock relative to a market average. It tells me nothing about whether I will lose money. In fact, the alpha is a better measure of a risky stock; a negative alpha, regardless of its volatility, suggests that the stock is performing worse than the market average. I will lose money on a poor-performing stock with a low alpha regardless of what level exists for its beta.

Diversification is also less than optimal for substantial profit. Diversification may lessen the effect of a losing position, but it also lessens the effect of a winning position. It's the "chicken" way of avoiding investment mistakes and avoiding the use of a tested, robust investment system. In a portfolio, because it is a business, meritocracy must rule. A portfolio should be filled with the strongest, most volatile stocks possible. If the oil stocks are the strongest, the portfolio should own nothing but oil stocks. If the oil and ditch-digging stocks are the strongest and most volatile, the only diversification should be in those two sectors. The purpose in portfolio management is to make money, not be average or equal to other portfolios. Risk should be controlled by risk management, not by diversification. In the market decline between 2007 and 2009, all stocks declined. Diversification was a useless method of controlling capital loss.

Exit Strategy

Exit strategies are risk-avoidance strategies. They are compiled to protect against capital loss or to lock in profits. Protecting against loss can be difficult. The standard method is to implement a *protective stop* underneath the entry price to protect against a large loss in case the entry decision was incorrect. This may protect a position against a single loss, but it doesn't protect against a string of losses, nor does it protect against a large drawdown due to poor portfolio management. A string of losses may result from a poor selection method or from a general market decline. Poor selection can be reduced through proper position sizing (never putting too much money at risk in any specific position) or by market timing when a broad signal on the market suggests stepping completely away from the market for a while.

Market timing is a problem that investment managers do not like to face. When market timing signals that it is time to sell stocks, because the majority of investors are optimistic about the markets, and their customers are members of the public, the pressure is heavy on the manager not to act on the market timing signal. These customers often pull their money out of a fund that is selling when the market is high and reduce the management fee on the assets being managed. At that time, the fund's sales department exerts pressure on the manager to keep the customers happy by remaining in the market even when professionally it is obvious the market is in trouble. Most funds don't allow market timing at all in their charter, thus forcing the manager into taking his lumps when the market declines. This conflict between the portfolio managers and sales department and customers also occurs at market bottoms as well when customers don't want to own stock at all, yet the opportunity exists for a large market rise. The relationship between bullish and bearish sentiment in the market and the market's future direction is an entire study of its own, but the rule of thumb is that when the public is overly optimistic, the market is at a top, and, conversely, when the public is overly pessimistic, the market is at a bottom. Public pressure from news, investor comments, TV, advisors, and other outside sources to conform to existing public opinion make a market timing signal very difficult to follow. It is one reason why superior results come from a disciplined algorithmic system that has proven to work in both types of markets and needs no emotional input.

Although the use of *price targets* is an exit strategy, I've not found any means of accurately projecting a price target. What I have found is that a price target can be deceiving. Invariably, either the price will fall short of the target, leaving the dilemma of when to sell, or it will exceed the target price by such a substantial amount that I feel foolish in having sold it so early. I don't believe in using price targets except as a technique for gauging the strength of a trend. This method is explained in Chapter 8, "Cycles and the Forward Line."

Money Management Strategy

This book is about proper investment and trading involving an entry strategy and an exit strategy. I highlight the best strategy that I have found and show how it has worked in the past and will likely work in the future. Money management strategy—how to organize a portfolio to reduce portfolio drawdown, as opposed to individual stock drawdown—is another subject, one I don't touch. I avoid it because it is complicated and deeply personal. What should the initial capital be, what should the trade size in shares or dollars be, should the strategy be combined with others and to what degree, what should the risk strategies and execution style be, what should the number of positions be, should leverage be used, and so on are all factors that should be addressed, though this is rarely done by portfolio managers and investors. I suggest that when you reach this stage in your investments study, you consult one of the excellent books on the subject. Don't be fooled by the constant use of the term *trader* in these books. The principles apply to any size portfolio, and most managers of large portfolios, being unaware of them, have difficulty in understanding why they consistently underperform the markets.

Books on Money Management and Position Sizing (In Alphabetical Order by Author)

Faith, Curtis. *Way of the Turtle: The Secret Methods That Turned Ordinary People into Legendary Traders*. New York, NY: McGraw-Hill, 2007.

Kaufman, Perry J. *Trading Systems and Methods*. 5th ed. New York, NY: John Wiley & Sons, Inc., 2013.

McDowell, Bennett A., and Steve Nison. *A Trader's Money Management System: How to Ensure Profit and Avoid Risk of Ruin*. New York, NY: John Wiley & Sons, Inc., 2008.

Penfold, Brent. *The Universal Principles of Successful Trading: Essential Knowledge for All Traders in All Markets*. New York, NY: John Wiley & Sons, Inc., 2010.

Schwager, Jack D., and Ed Seykota. *Hedge Fund Market Wizards: How Winning Traders Win*. New York, NY: John Wiley & Sons, Inc., 2012.

Tharp, Van K. *Super Trader, Expanded Edition: Make Consistent Profits in Good and Bad Markets*. 2nd ed. New York, NY: McGraw-Hill, 2010.

Tharp, Van K. *Van Tharp's Definitive Guide to Position Sizing*. New York, NY: McGraw-Hill, 2008.

Vince, Ralph. *The Handbook of Portfolio Mathematics: Formulas for Optimal Allocation and Leverage*. New York, NY: John Wiley & Sons, Inc., 2007.

Vince, Ralph. *Risk-Opportunity Analysis*. CreateSpace Independent Publishing Platform, 2012.

Backtesting—Standard and Walk-Forward Optimization

The results in this book are from standard and walk-forward optimizations I performed at the end of the year 2012. The data is the daily closing price of all U.S. common stocks traded from 1990 through 2012. The data includes listed and delisted stocks during that period, to eliminate survivor bias, but is limited to operating companies. The numerous derivative issues such as Exchange Traded Funds (ETFs) and other interest-rate related stocks are excluded. (ETFs are used in the trading section beginning in Chapter 6.) The total number of stocks analyzed is 6,272. The list also includes American Depository Receipts (for stocks traded in foreign stock markets) and other forms of foreign stock replications that are listed in each of the three principal exchanges: the New York Stock Exchange, the American Stock Exchange, and the NASDAQ exchange. Price data is adjusted for splits and capital distributions but not for dividend payments. I use only price in this system because, as technicians have long argued, price includes every aspect of a stock's value, its history, its emotional appeal, and its place in the world as of each trade.

Standard Optimization

A *standard optimization* tests results from many variable parameters (such as lookback period in relative strength, rank to buy, and rank to sell) to see which combination gives the "best" answer. The best answer is subject to the preference of the analyst and is usually a combination of profit and potential loss. The final objective, called the *objective function,* is the statistic by which each test is measured. The highest level of objective function is the best answer. For example, suppose I use net profit as the objective function. As the computer runs through the various parameter combinations, it will arrive at a "best" set of parameters that gives the highest net profit of all the systems. This would then be the best system based on net profit as an objective function. Of course, net profit alone doesn't account for risk. The MAR ratio then could become the objective function. This is a ratio between compounded annual growth rate percentage (CAGR) and maximum drawdown percentage (MDD). The series of tests for optimal parameters can then select the combination that had the highest MAR ratio. There are many other objective functions that can be used depending on the result that is important to the analyst.

Walk-Forward Optimization

In a walk-forward optimization, the optimization process is similar to the standard method in that it also uses an objective function by which the results of each optimization are measured. It is different, however, in that it optimizes over shorter periods called "runs" within the entire data series and then tests the parameters found to be the best in the short period on a selected portion of the data that is independent and thus "unknown" to the optimization data. It summarizes these "out of sample (OOS)" results to see how well the best combinations from the original data worked in the unknown data. A successful result is a return in the unknown data similar to the return in the known data. In the walk-forward optimization the number of runs is varied to be sure no pattern has been present between time periods, and the percentage of out-of-sample data used in the tests is varied to be sure that the results summarize both long and short periods subsequent to the optimizations. The process of optimizing and testing results in unknown data is thus to see if the original system hypothesis has merit. One that has a high percentage of favorable test results is called "robust." It has a high chance of continuing to profit in the future.

Book Organization

Now that you have made it through the introduction, this book becomes more specific with its tests of the relative strength investment system and several trading systems. Each of the following chapters explains the concept of the study starting with what backtesting and methods I use, followed by the results and graphs of the studies themselves. In the investment section, the results include the best lookback period for relative price strength, the rank or ratio for portfolio addition or deletion, the minimum volume and price for an initial trade, and the percent stop that produces the best results in tests with data unknown to the study. I then cover derived relative strength system rules and modify them with a market-timing system to reduce the effects of a market decline. The final results are practical, robust stock picking investment systems and technical trading systems that should not tax the abilities of the individual investor and can be applied to any size portfolio.

Endnotes

1. Pardo, Robert. *The Evaluation and Optimization of Trading Strategies*. Hoboken, NJ: John Wiley & Sons, Inc., 2008.

2. Kirkpatrick, Charles D. *Beat the Market: Invest by Knowing What Stocks to Buy and What Stocks to Sell*. Upper Saddle River, NJ: FT Press, 2009.

3. O'Shaughnessy, James P. *What Works on Wall Street: The Classic Guide to the Best-Performing Investment Strategies of All Time*. New York, NY: McGraw-Hill, 2012.

2

Investment Strategies: Backtesting

In the world of trading market systems development, backtesting is the primary means of determining the optimal set of rules and results for any newly developed algorithmic system. Backtesting can be accomplished in three ways. In order of their reliability and, thus, usefulness for a proposed system, they are a single backtest, a standard optimization, and a walk-forward optimization.

A *single backtest* occurs when the analyst has already developed a reasonable hypothesis, usually from other tests, and wants to see if the parameters still hold. An example is shown in Figure 2.1, an equity curve graph of the profitability of my original formula for using only relative price strength to buy and sell stocks. The upward slope of the equity curve indicates that the strategy still makes money; notice also that the equity curve is not smooth and is interrupted by several large and lengthy declines or drawdowns. This high-risk profile makes the system suspect. Indeed, it needs a complete revamping.

Standard optimization is used when a hypothesis is being developed. It uses a broad range of data in a set of rules to see if any of the contiguous series of parameters produce a profitable result. If successful, the optimization establishes specific ranges of profitable parameters for later testing. The results of optimization, however, should never be used straightaway without further testing in unknown data. Optimization fits the formula to the data, but the resulting system may have no predictive value. The advantage of optimization is that it runs through a large data sample and provides a less cumbersome report on whether the proposed system has merit. It also eliminates those parameter combinations that show poor or negative results. If the optimization shows a profit in a majority of the parameter combinations, it may be a good system. If it doesn't, no further study is necessary, and its hypothesis can be discarded.

Once a profitable hypothesis is found and a suitable range of parameter values has been culled from the data, *walk-forward optimization* optimizes the potential system using the previously determined range of parameters and then tests the results in unknown data. It fine-tunes the system and, if successful, produces a system that will presumably work in the future. This final optimization is where most systems fail. Finding a system that has worked in the past is easy; finding one that will work in the future is difficult.

Standard Optimization

Optimization is the process by which an analyst hypothesizes and tests a *set of rules* for investing or trading in the market. The rules can be an indicator or series of indicators, but it is advisable to keep the set relatively simple. The more complicated the set of rules, the more likely that a change in the future markets will upset future performance. Also, the more complicated the formula, the more difficult it is to find the right parameters. All rules have variables, numbers that define the formulas and provide the eventual system. *Parameters* are the actual values of the variables used in the rules. Optimization takes a range of parameters for the variables proposed in the system and tests them to see which combination provides the best results.

Relative Strength Rules

Relative strength is a stock selection process that argues that the strongest stocks are the best future performers. It is controversial because it negates the efficient markets hypothesis that states that past price performance has no predictive value. There are numerous methods of calculating relative price strength. The academics have mostly used price change comparisons over specific time intervals. Professionals have used price comparisons to market averages or to specific industry groups of stocks. I use a relative strength rule that calculates the ratio of the current closing price to a moving average of the closing prices. This method avoids the problems associated with market averages, includes all stocks in whatever universe I choose, and avoids the "drop-off effect" from comparing one price with another over time. The ratio is then ranked against the same ratio for every other stock in the data (6,272) and converted into a percentile whereby the ratios in the top 1% are ranked 99, the next 1% are ranked 98, and so on through the entire file. The rules are to buy a stock when its rank rises to a certain rank, the buy rank, and if owned, to sell it when its rank declines to a certain rank, the sell rank. The variables are, thus, the length of the moving average in the ratio, the buy rank, and the sell rank. The parameters are the potential values used in the optimization.

The closing price is provided by the data used in the optimization, but the length of the moving average (the *lookback*) is a variable because it can be any of a number of days, weeks, hours, and so on. Using a range of possible parameters for the lookback, combined with the range of possible buy and sell ranks, the optimization finds the "best" of these parameters. The calculation and ranking are done once a day, but the performance index is calculated once a week when stocks are added or deleted based on the relative strength ranks for that week. The reason for calculating the ranks once a day, even though the addition and deletion is based on relative strength weekly, is that other price-related stops may trigger within a week and must be recorded on the day and price that they occur.

Walk-Forward Optimization

Walk-forward optimization uses the same optimization method as the standard optimization, only it keeps some of the price data separate to be used in later testing of the optimization results. After optimizing a section of the data, the method uses this "unknown" data called *out of sample* (OOS) data to test the parameters derived from the optimization. It then progresses to another section and repeats the process of optimization and testing on unknown data. Finally, when all the sections have been completed, the resulting performance in the unknown data of all the sections is analyzed for "robustness," a fancy word that means solidity and dependability. If the optimized data produces parameters that do not provide robustness, then they must be discarded. They don't work, and likely the entire formula doesn't work. This is the usual case in sifting through formulas to find the best for a certain market and can be time consuming and discouraging. In the relative strength model, however, I know it works because it has worked in past live use, but I don't know the ideal parameters or the special nuances necessary to make it a super system. That knowledge will come as the current study progresses. So let's begin the process with deciding which data to use and what parameter range to test.

Equity Curve

An *equity curve* is a semilogarithmic plot in time of the performance of the strategy's net profit (gross profit minus gross loss). An equity curve is the first summary that a systems analyst investigates. An equity curve represents how the hypothetical account would have performed over the test period using the derived parameters. A successful system generates a rising profit line with a minimum number of corrections called *drawdowns*. The shape of the curve will be smooth and steadily upward to the right. Additional information and measures are necessary for a full determination of a strategy's robustness, but all analysis begins with an equity curve. It immediately tells the analyst whether the strategy has promise.

Is an equity curve predictive? Is it useful for determining the future of the system? The analyst doesn't know. All he knows is that the derived parameters worked in the past. The future may be different; it usually is. So the parameters derived from the optimization may not work in the future. Why is this?

When the best parameters are sought, the optimization process looks for those parameters that provide the best result. A standard optimization uses only past data. It, therefore, reflects only the past and not the future. It shows what could have been had you been prescient enough at the beginning of the study to choose the correct parameters, but it says nothing about how the system parameters will work in the future. Thus, for confidence in the ability of the system to work in the future, the future must be estimated by either leaving past data out of the optimization to use later in tests of the parameters, as is done in walk-forward optimization, or running the system "live" in the actual future to see if it works.

For the parameters in the relative strength system I mentioned earlier, I ran the system live for more than 23 years. It was a long wait to see if the system worked, especially when using weekly data. Figure 2.1 is the equity curve for how the system worked since 1990 using the data available for this study. It is the result of recalculating the equity curve from a 182-day lookback, a 97 buy rank, and a 52 sell rank, the parameters used during that period, and reassembling the results into an equal-dollar-weighted index of the 1,002 stocks in the current sample database (see the "Sample Database Size" section in Chapter 3, "Initial Standard Optimizations").

The equity curve demonstrates the several reasons why determination of the best parameters is necessary. The general direction of the curve is upward and to the right as it should be. However, it is marked by a number of large corrections. Finally, while the compound annual growth rate was 19.57%, a very high number compared with all market averages, the rate of growth was slow during the early years from 1990 through 1994 and slowed considerably in the last five years.

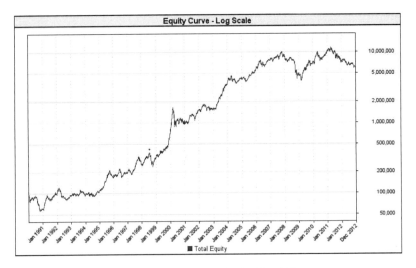

Created using Trading Blox Builder 4.1x64 © 2003 Trading Blox, LLC

Figure 2.1   Equity curve—Equal-dollar-weighted index of stocks selected from a database of 1,002 stocks from January 1, 1990, through December 31, 2012, using the original relative strength formula from the book *Beat the Market.*

Equity Curve Overfitting

Optimization has its flaws, most of which can be corrected. Many analysts believe that optimizations are nothing but quantifications of the past and have no predictive value. This is true when the optimization is done poorly and without regard for proper and thorough walk-forward analysis. Most unsuccessful systems have an overly reliant dependence on past history alone. It is an obstacle that the analyst must constantly be aware of and prevent from entering his calculations.

Because markets oscillate and because it is the timing of these oscillations that makes money from the markets, the desire is to see if those oscillations can be predicted. If those oscillation predictions could be projected into the future based on the curve fitting of the past, money could be made. The problem is that the more the markets are fitted to a mathematical curve, the less likely they are to follow the derived formula. The reason is that the market is a dynamic entity, always changing, always doing the unexpected. Thus, a system should not be so precise that it attempts to anticipate every minor turn, but should be flexible enough to adjust to the market's vagaries. The more the optimization is fine-tuned to the history of market prices, the greater the danger that it becomes useless as a predictive device. The market is not a trajectory into space, or a combustion engine, each of which follow strict principles of physics. It is like smoke in that its precise projection is almost impossible to anticipate. The more it is studied as a physics problem, the more likely that any outcome will be flawed. To combat this tendency, the good analyst uses a long chain of raw data that has occurred through multiple changes in market behavior. He doesn't add variable after variable to the system to make it fit the past market. Searching for the perfect fit is based on the erroneous belief that future results will be predictable from the derived formula. Rather than deciding on the system parameters based on the perfect fitting to past data, the good analyst, using optimization as a beginning, decides the final system parameters based on how they act in unknown data, data that has never been used in the model building. After all, the purpose in a system is to behave profitably in unknown data in the future. Deriving the parameters only from past data is missing the point.

To combat the evils of curve fitting, the following paraphrases what Pardo (292) suggests as preventive measures:

1. Limit degrees of freedom (few variables and many data points).
2. Increase the amount of raw data to cover different market conditions and generate many trades (50 minimum).
3. Use correct optimization methods.
4. Discard big single wins in small trade samples.
5. Use walk-forward analysis tests for robustness.

Entry Strategy

All systems require an entry and exit strategy. Although the exit strategy is likely the most important, the entry strategy cannot be neglected and usually consists of the set of rules that define the system. Exit strategies are generally limited to broad methods of protecting against capital loss and protecting existing profits. Thus, although important, exit strategies are often common across different systems.

For reliability of results, a system must generate a large number of trades to avoid the statistical problem of not enough samples. A set of rules that generates only a few trades requires either more data or a shorter time interval between data points. In the singular run of my earlier relative strength system shown in Figure 2.1, there were 9,197 trades. Usually only a few hundred are necessary, but the more there are, the more confident the analyst can be with the results.

In addition to the rules for the entry strategy that derive from some formula or investment theory, certain practical aspects of an entry strategy must also be considered. These are the nature of the investments themselves, specifically whether initial price and/or initial trading volume are important to the results. In theory, each is an important consideration in technical systems, but they are rarely tested for accuracy and actual effect. In the next chapter, I look at these additional considerations to the entry strategy for this system, and find that, surprisingly, initial price has little effect on the performance of the system, and initial volume only a minor effect.

Exit Strategy May Affect Results

Most optimization is done on entry strategies and leaves the exit strategy to some standard formula, often just a holding period in time. Using just a holding period, however, introduces other factors into the model. How long should the holding period be? This is a variable that can affect the performance results of the entry strategy. Suppose the test occurs just before a market decline. Does the exit strategy adjust for varying holding periods? Does the exit strategy explain the poor performance of the entry strategy? You can see that the exit strategy has its effect on the results no matter what it is. It must be flexible enough to only have a minimal effect on the entry strategy. So what does the analyst do?

In this study, I am fortunate in that the entry and exit strategies use the same variable—relative price strength. The basic formula is simple: Buy when a stock reaches a certain level or rank and sell it when it declines to a certain level or rank. This avoids the question of time entirely because those stocks that end their upward run (suggested by the high relative price strength) may falter at any time and be eliminated solely on their relative price rank or level regardless of the time in the portfolio.

Figure 2.2 shows the arithmetic scale of the equity curve and below it the percentage drawdowns from prior index peaks. The maximum drawdown (MDD) is 61.3%, a level far beyond what the average investor is able to withstand. In addition to the large drawdown, the longest "underwater" period, the period between the last high and a new high, is 38 weeks. How many investors can still believe in a system that loses that percentage and that takes so long to recover, despite the eventual excellent performance? Not many. As mentioned in Chapter 1, "Introduction," the parameters for this system were determined more than thirty years ago. Fortunately, the system generally was profitable and had an annual compound return of 19.57%.

The exit strategy solution to fighting drawdowns is solved with two methods. The first is the exit strategy on individual investments, and the second is the use of a market-timing model to reduce the effect of overall market declines. The individual relative strength exit strategy in a market decline will often be late in ridding the portfolio of declining stocks. To combat this drawdown problem, I tested the use of a percent protective stop on individual issues.

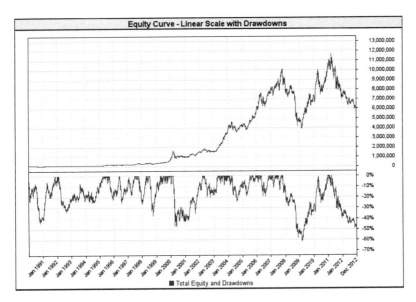

Created using Trading Blox Builder 4.1x64 © 2003 Trading Blox, LLC

Figure 2.2   Arithmetic equity curve and percent drawdowns—Equal-dollar-weighted index of stocks selected from a database of 1,002 stocks from January 1, 1990, through December 31, 2012, using the original relative strength formula from the book *Beat the Market*.

The market decline drawdown is fought differently. Figure 2.2 shows three periods when the equity curve lost more than 40%. They were in 1990–1991, 2000–2001, and 2008–2009. These periods were times of major market corrections. A general market correction essentially takes all stocks with it. Strong relative strength stocks still decline, and when deleted from the list, they are replaced by other strong stocks that in turn also decline and are deleted. This means that protective stops on individual stocks will be ineffective during a market decline. The only way to fight this problem is to have a market-timing method that shuts down the system during market declines and reopens the system once a market bottom has been reached. A market-timing model using a series of moving-average crossovers to stop the system entirely when the overall market looks weak and to reenter when the market improves its own upward momentum is the usual solution to market timing. A market-timing add-on is included in the final model in Chapter 5, "Stock Selection Using Relative Strength."

Equal-Dollar Weighted Index

Performance of investment systems can be made complicated by including too many variables unrelated to the system itself. Most optimizations are completed on a hypothetical portfolio of stocks with a specified and limited number of holdings. When a portfolio is first organized, it is easy to decide how large the positions should be by dividing the value of the portfolio by the number of stocks allowed. For example, in a portfolio of $1,000,000 with an investment limit of 20 stocks, each initial stock position would be $50,000 ($1,000,000 divided by 20). As time goes on, however, the change in position sizes, through differences in the performance of separate stocks, complicates the performance results by overly emphasizing the successful stocks to the disadvantage of the unsuccessful ones. Because new positions are added to the portfolio when they fit the selection criteria of the system, and others are deleted from the portfolio in response to an exit strategy, the remaining portfolio is a mess of differently weighted stocks. The portfolio becomes a complex problem of weighting new positions, reallocation, and what to do with remaining cash from sales not large enough for a standard new position.

An additional difficulty with using a standard portfolio model to test an investment method is that the limit to the number of positions may arbitrarily exclude stocks that qualify but are restricted from admission by the number of the positions already existing. If 50 stocks qualify, for example, and the portfolio is limited to 30 stocks, 20 of which are already involved, only 10 are allowed in as new stocks.

Forty are bypassed. Thus, the results of the portfolio don't reflect the performance of all the stocks that met the qualifications for admission.

Ideally, the portfolio should not be limited in the number of positions, and all positions should be equally weighted. The correct portfolio should be resized at a standard interval to minimize the effect on its performance by one or two especially significant stocks with large gains. On the resizing, every position should readjust to an equal dollar amount. This type of hypothetical portfolio is called an *equal-dollar-weighted index*.

An equal-dollar-weighted index takes any number of stocks that meet the membership criteria (like a specific relative strength rank) and equally weights them by dollars per position. It reapportions all positions each week, making each equally dollar weighted, and an unlimited number of stocks can be added or deleted. For example, a $1,000,000 portfolio/index may include 500 stocks that meet the membership criteria. For the first week, the hypothetical position size of each would begin at $2,000 per stock. Say this index increased 3% to $1,030,000 over the following week. At the week's end, newly qualified stocks are added and other stocks are deleted from the index. Suppose the index ends up with 450 stocks, some from the earlier list that were not deleted, plus some from new stocks, and minus those that were deleted. For the second week, the value of each stock position is reallocated to $2,228.90 per stock ($1,030,000 divided by the 450 stocks now in the index). Each active position is thus resized by adding or subtracting (buying or selling) enough shares at the then current price to equalize all positions in the index to $2,228.90. This process is continued each week until the end of the entire test period. The performance of the index becomes a relatively pure expression of the investment method being tested. It measures the average gain or loss of each stock added to the portfolio using the entry and exit rules alone. If, after testing a large number of parameter combinations in the rules, one system using one set of parameters produces a better result than another, it is likely a better system. Only the additions and deletions to the index have influenced the end result.

Should resizing and additions, deletions, and readjustments include slippage and commissions? My answer is "No." The equal-dollar-weighted index is designed to show the success or failure of the system alone. It is not a portfolio. No money would ever be run on a portfolio that adjusted its positions so rapidly. Slippage and commissions are a portfolio management problem and are irrelevant to the stock selections system. Eventually, they may be found to severely limit the profits of a stock selection system to the point where it is not robust as a portfolio system, but introducing commissions and slippage at the early stage, as important as they ultimately are to portfolio management, only adds variables not related to the system itself.

Objective Function

To test any investment method, the analyst must have a specific goal in mind to focus the optimization upon. This target is called an *objective function*. The analyst looks for the set of parameters that is the best as determined by the objective function. The term *best* is used to determine the system that is most desirable and robust. *Best* in systems study is the highest rank of each trial in terms of the objective function.

What is the function that will provide the best system? There is no easy answer because systems analysts look for many characteristics in their search for a profitable, robust system. Most analysts know what they want in the way of a system. The basics are a high profit and a low risk of capital loss. To quantify this into a function is partially subjective. Aside from profit and avoidance of loss, other factors might be of interest to the analyst, such as a short holding period, frequency of trading, absolute rather than relative gain, a high average win-to-loss ratio, and the Sharpe ratio, or what is called the "Ulcer Index" (square root of the sum of squared drawdowns/number of bars). It can be net profit, for example, but net profit doesn't include the risk of capital loss. It can be drawdown, but drawdown doesn't account for net profit.

The most common objective function measures profit versus capital risk. I use the MAR ratio of compound annual growth rate divided by the maximum drawdown. It is easily calculated and gives a reasonable idea of the overall value of the system.

The other group of objective functions has to do with fitting the actual equity curve, which includes all profits and drawdowns, to an ideal. I have used the *R-squared method (R2)*, which gives a statistical reading of the amount that the equity curve approximates a straight regression line drawn from the beginning of the equity curve to its end.

Another equity-curve-fit objective function method is called the *Perfect Profit Correlation (PPC)*. This method takes every buy and sell execution for every stock in the index and relates it to what would have happened had the actual low and peak in each stock been used instead of the actual signals. It is, thus, a measure of how the system performed against what would have been the ideal. In this exercise, because the number of stocks is large and, thus, the number of transactions is large, approaching 10,000 round-trip trades, the calculation is prohibitive. The R-squared method accomplished much the same result and is much easier to calculate.

Objective functions should never be optimized themselves nor should they be changed from test to test. A comparison between results is meaningless when the objective function is different for each. At the end of the optimization, the analyst has the best set of parameters for his set of rules and objective function. That doesn't mean that he should immediately call his broker and begin trading that model, however. There are many obstacles to overcome yet.

Procedure Followed in This Study

The process that follows in the next several chapters is composed of several important steps:

1. **Establish database integrity**—Daily stock price data for the past 30 years is downloaded from CSI (www.csi.com) for all active U.S. common stocks and American depository receipts (ADRs), excluding interest-related and derivative issues, preferred, units, warrants, and any other security not representing direct ownership in an operating company.

2. **Eliminate useless combinations of parameters**—A standard optimization is conducted of possible parameters for all basic variables (weekly lookback period, relative strength buy rank, relative strength sell rank) using MAR as the objective function. This leaves a range of parameters in each basic variable that may have predictive value.

3. **Determine best combinations of parameters**—A walk-forward optimization is conducted on the possible parameters using MAR as the objective function.

4. **Determine the best final system parameter combination**—Analyze the systems derived from the walk-forward optimization based on a series of ratios that provide insight into the robustness of the systems.

5. **Test and analyze other variables**—After the final robust system is determined, if such exists, experiment with variables such as percentage stop, initial price and/or volume, and market timing to see if the results are improved, and if so to use the derived parameters of the robust variables in the final model.

3

Initial Standard Optimizations

Starting now, I get into the boring subject of tests, numbers, statistics, and optimization method. Before the walk-forward optimizations, I must reduce the range of possible parameters in the study to cut down on processing time. Walk-forward optimization takes a large number of parameters and combs through them numerous times. For example, in this project, the minimum number of calculations, if we use only round numbers, is 100 rank numbers for buys in the index × 100 rank numbers for sells from the index × 251 trading days per year × 23 years of price history × 6,272 stocks × 30 lookback periods × 10 minimum volume trials × 30 percentage-stop levels × 9 walk-forward optimizations = $2.94455 \times e^{16}$ calculations if the entire range of possible parameters is studied. Needless to say, this would take a long time on a PC, even on a thousand PCs. But I don't need all the calculations because I already know several things. The first is that the buy rank is going to be relatively high, say somewhere between 90 and 99. This alone reduces the number of calculations by a factor of 90. I also know that the sell rank is going to be less than the buy rank and likely greater than 50; this reduces the calculations by a factor of 60. I know, too, that the lookback period will be longer than just a few weeks but not the full range.

To reduce the range and make the eventual walk-forward optimization less tedious, I perform standard optimizations on the data for each variable and look at the past history of the lookback, the buy rank, the sell rank, the stop loss percentage, the minimum initial volume, and the minimum initial price to find more specific and smaller ranges to use in the final optimizations. Each parameter is studied individually to reduce the odds that I am curve fitting the data. Curve fitting is more likely if I run the entire combination of parameters in one single run. In addition, I use statistical sampling methods to reduce the number of stocks in the walk-forward optimizations. These are particularly lengthy processes and are unaffected, within certain limits, by reducing the number of stocks to a 95% confidence level and 3% confidence interval.

Degrees of Freedom

The statistical term *degrees of freedom* is used to describe the reliability of a statistical test as it is related to the amount of data used. It is a term that differs in use between various scientific communities, but for this purpose, degrees of freedom is the total amount of data less the data needed to perform one complete set of calculations plus the number of rules applied to those calculations for the eventual result. It is the number of useful data that can be used for estimation. The theory basically states that the more data used in a statistical study, the more reliable the results. There is one joke among generally humorless statisticians about the husband who argues that because he has only one wife and she allows no degrees of freedom, he is entitled to increase his degrees of freedom by expanding his interests in other women.

A rule of thumb for degrees of freedom is that the database should be no less than 10 times the amount of data needed for the calculations and rules. In this study, the degrees of freedom at most is 380, the 376.5 trading days (longest possible lookback is 1 1/2 years at 251 trading days per year) plus 3 calculations (relative strength rank, ratio buy rule, and sell rule). The rule of thumb requires ten times this number for the minimum number of data points required for this study to satisfy the rule of degrees of freedom or 3,800 data points.

The actual number is 23 years times 251 trading days for each stock or 5,773 data points per stock, about one and a half times the minimum necessary number. I use 365 days per year rather than 251 trading days because the computer must account for each day whether it is a trading day or not in order to limit the weekly results to an even 7 days each week.

Once the ranges for the lookback period have been defined more precisely later in this chapter, the necessary degrees of freedom decline to 283, and the ratio of data available to what is needed rises to more than twice what is necessary.

Sample Database Size

Stock market studies are notoriously inaccurate. This inaccuracy allows me to reduce the number of calculations by taking a sample of the whole database for the various and laborious tests without sacrificing relative accuracy. This is the same principle as that used in political polling. Only a fraction of the total population is polled, and the results are still accurate within a certain degree of confidence. Table 3.1 shows the various confidence intervals at standard 95% and 99% confidence levels. For my purposes, a 95% confidence level and a 3% confidence interval is more than satisfactory. This means I can have 95% confidence that results of the calculations are accurate to within 3%. As an example, if I find a system that produces compound annual growth rate (CAGR) of 24% per year, I can be 95% confident that the system return is accurate to 24 +/- 0.72—that is, between 23.28% and 24.72%. The advantage, of course, in using sample data is that it reduces the computer processing by almost 65%. I thus adjust the number of stocks in the study to one sixth of the original 6,272 to 1,002 stocks, which gives me a confidence level of 95% and an interval of less than 3%. Later, I can run the full database with the derived system to make sure that the sampling did not influence the results.

Table 3.1   Sample Sizes for a Population of 6,272 Stocks

Confidence Interval/Confidence Level	95%	99%
1%	3,794	4,555
2%	1,737	2,501
3%	912	1,428

Lookback

The *lookback* is the time the formula looks back in time to calculate the simple moving average used in the ratio of relative strength. In my earlier book, the lookback was assumed to be 26 weeks (6 months) or 182 calendar days. This figure emerged out of Robert Levy's[1] original work on relative strength. It was used later in his book on the subject,[2] and by me in my work. Levy had told me that he had experimented with lookback periods because they were crucial to the determination of the most profitable relative strength ratio. His work, he said, showed that 26 weeks produced the best profits (no consideration for risk of loss at that time), that 52 weeks also showed excellent profits but not as high as using 26 weeks, and that anything less than 6 weeks had a negative return. In other words, the short-term relative strength figures were counterproductive and caused losses.

To retest his suggestion of lookback period using MAR (CAGR divided by the maximum drawdown [MDD]) as an objective function to adjust for drawdown risk, I run a standard optimization using the original parameters for the variables of buy and sell rank and vary the parameter for lookback to between 91 and 546 calendar days (13 and 78 weeks). This optimization covers the period January 1, 1990, through December 31, 2012, and uses all 1,002 stocks in the sample database. The optimization process, using the standard rules of buying at a specific relative strength rank and selling at another specific relative strength rank, creates the equal-dollar-weighted index of stocks that simulates an equally weighted portfolio, and measures the performance of that index for each of the different lookback periods. The process progresses step-by-step through each potential weekly lookback from the first week (91st day) through the 546th day, and produces a graph of the MAR ratio of the equal-dollar-weighted index for each of the lookback weeks. Figure 3.1 shows the important results.

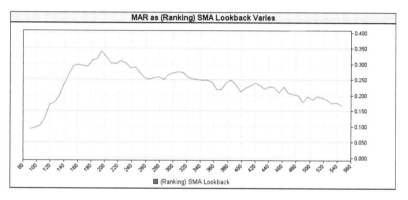

Created using Trading Blox Builder 4.1x64 © 2003 Trading Blox, LLC

Figure 3.1   Step graph of lookback periods 91 through 546 days compared with MAR results on 1,002 stocks—January 1, 1990, through December 31, 2012.

Figure 3.1 shows a sharp rise in performance to the "smooth hump" in the area between 161 days (23 weeks) and 231 days (33 weeks) and a gradual dwindling thereafter. The peak MAR is at 196 days (28 weeks). As Levy's original work showed, the shorter lookback periods have extremely low performance results. Be aware. Some publicly available relative strength services use short lookback periods in their calculations, an obvious mistake that proves they have not tested their work.

A "smooth hump" in the results is very favorable for further study. It demonstrates that the results are not easily affected by changes on the variable's parameter. These results for the lookback show only a minor difference in MAR during the period of the hump. Should market conditions change and the lookback period also change, I can feel confident that the results will remain essentially the same. On the other hand, sharp peaks and valleys in a step graph show that using different parameters gives erratic results. It implies that a change in the parameter due to a market change would have very different results in portfolio performance, thus decreasing the system's reliability and robustness. Smooth humps are good.

Buy Rank

The *buy rank* is the rank that the stock must reach to become a member of the equal-dollar-weighted index, the hypothetical portfolio I use to measure performance. Traditionally, I have used 97% or above as the buy rank. Figure 3.2 shows the step graph of the MAR results for using a buy rank between 90% and 99%. The standard optimization uses the 1,002-stock database and holds the sell rank steady at the original 52% and the lookback steady at the original 26 weeks.

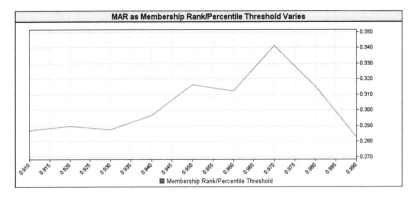

Created using Trading Blox Builder 4.1x64 © 2003 Trading Blox, LLC

Figure 3.2   Step graph of relative strength buy rank percentile 20% through 99% compared with MAR results on 1,002 stocks—January 1, 1990, through December 31, 2012.

I believe the graph clearly shows the ideal zone of parameters to optimize for the system. The equity curve graph shows a steady climb in MAR from a relative strength rank of 90% through to 97%. The best result is at 97% with a MAR almost reaching 0.34. For those who doubt the value of relative price strength as a stock selection method, this chart should dispel any such thoughts. While counterintuitive to those who believe in buying weakness, there is no question that the higher the strength of a stock, the better it performs when adjusted for risk of drawdown. The exception seems to be for those stocks with ranks greater than 97%. 98% is the upper limit before the MAR declines to below all other levels in the chart. I thus use the range of 95% to 98% for the optimization runs of the ranking system.

Sell Rank

The *sell rank* is the rank below which a stock must reach to be deleted from the index. This was first optimized while holding the membership rank and lookback steady, and the results are shown in Figure 3.3. The graph shows that a peak occurs around 59% and the range is between 59% and 61%. There are several "humps" in the chart, one at the low percentages around 50% and another at the higher range of 79%. The earlier hump is affected by stocks that have turned low enough not to recover, and the higher hump is affected by stocks that are sold at opportune levels but in some cases too early. It obviously is not helpful to sell stocks on their first sign of weakness from a high level of relative strength. The performance numbers decline rapidly from a sell percentage of 79% and above. I often receive questions from customers about having the sell rank so low (I used 52% historically) and asking if it would not be wiser to sell stocks on the first sign of weakness. The chart shows the story of why you must hold onto stocks through periods of weakness until the weakness becomes serious below the high 50% range. The range I use for optimizations is from 58% through 61%.

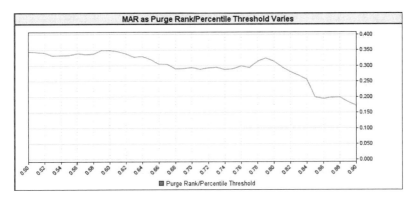

Created using Trading Blox Builder 4.1x64 © 2003 Trading Blox, LLC

Figure 3.3   Step graph of relative strength sell rank percentile 50% through 90% compared with MAR results on 1,002 stocks—January 1, 1990, through December 31, 2012.

Percent Protective Stop

Percent stops are sell orders placed at the purchase of a stock to be executed if the stock price declines from the entry price by a certain percentage. It does not prevent drawdown because drawdown is usually due to a successive series of losses. However, it does cull a portfolio of stocks that are potentially damaging and thus saves capital in individual positions. It is called a *protective stop* because it protects invested capital from loss and provides a measurement of risk that can be later used to determine position size.

The question is what percentage protective stop should be used? The larger the percentage, the more difficult the climb back to parity, and the smaller the percentage the more likely the stock will be sold prematurely. The best level is subject to testing, and Figure 3.4 shows the standard optimization of the percent stop for all trades over the 23-year period between 0% and 30% stop. The graph continues upward with no apparent peak. The higher MAR ratios occur at the higher percentage stops. Not until the percentage test is extended in Figure 3.5 to 50% is there a peak. It appears at a percentage stop level of 42%, which is ridiculous and would be unacceptable to most investors to have to wait for a 42% loss before selling a position.

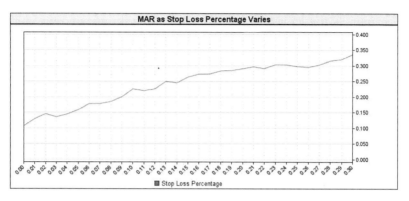

Created using Trading Blox Builder 4.1x64 © 2003 Trading Blox, LLC

Figure 3.4 Step graph of stop loss percentage for individual stocks from 0% to 30% compared with MAR results on 1,002 stocks—January 1, 1990, through December 31, 2012.

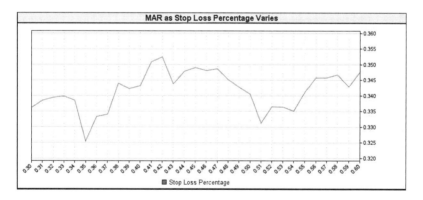

Created using Trading Blox Builder 4.1x64 © 2003 Trading Blox, LLC

Figure 3.5 Step graph of stop loss percentage for individual stocks from 0% to 30% compared with MAR results on 1,002 stocks—January 1, 1990, through December 31, 2012.

If we are trying to limit loss to something reasonable, say 20%, a 42% stop is meaningless. The evidence thus suggests that a percentage stop is not going to help in performance, and for that reason it is no longer considered in any models.

Initial 50-Day Trading Volume

In the initial walk-forward optimizations, I concentrate on the basics, namely the lookback, the buy rank, the sell rank, and the stop loss. Additional constraints are sometimes useful either to improve the performance results or to introduce practicality. In the case of initial volume, the reason for its inclusion is practical. Most institutions and individuals cannot buy and sell penny stocks or illiquid stocks that trade a few shares a day. By screening for minimum acceptable volume, that practical problem is avoided, but the question then is whether restricting initial volume adversely affects performance.

Limiting trading volume is really a consideration for portfolio management because its influence is focused on the liquidity of the purchase, something that might be limited by the size of the portfolio it is bound for. But as Figure 3.6 shows, the highest MAR is achieved when trading volume is small. The peak in the MAR occurs at a 50-day average of 10,000 shares and declines thereafter. There appears to be no advantage for purchasing anything less than 10,000 because all MAR ratios for volume above 10,000 shares are higher than any step graph before. 10,000 shares seem to be the limit below which calculations can be discarded and will thus be a standard screen in the final optimizations.

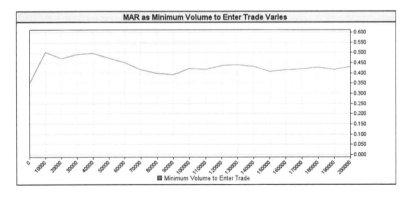

Created using Trading Blox Builder 4.1x64 © 2003 Trading Blox, LLC

Figure 3.6   Step graph of 50-day average minimum trading volume for individual stocks from 0 shares to 200,000 shares compared with MAR results on 1,002 stocks—January 1, 1990, through December 31, 2012.

Initial 50-Day Average Price

The other potential limiting factor often considered in an entry strategy is the minimum price of the stock. Most margin requirements limit margin to stocks with a value of $5 or more, and most institutional investors can only buy stocks with market capitalization above a certain amount. Thus, the practical problem for this study is whether to test all stocks in the database or just those that have reached above a certain price determined by a standard optimization test. The latter is performed first, and the results are shown in Figure 3.7.

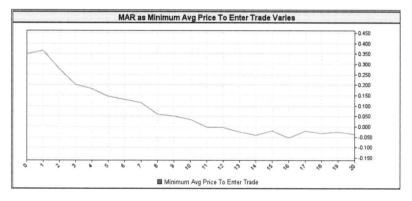

Created using Trading Blox Builder 4.1x64 © 2003 Trading Blox, LLC

Figure 3.7   Step graph of 50-day average minimum stock price compared with MAR results on 1,002 stocks—January 1, 1990, through December 31, 2012.

When I use back-adjusted data, which has been adjusted for earlier stock splits and distributions, the computer takes the adjusted price rather than the actual price at the time of the reading. Thus, Microsoft stock, for example, has an adjusted price of 60 cents during 1900 and would be eliminated on any filter for stock price above $1. The results in Figure 3.7, therefore, are deceiving because they include stocks like Microsoft that have been back-adjusted. Nevertheless, the results show that a minimum stock price filter is counterproductive. The MAR declines steadily from no filter through a filter of

$20. Even with the problem of back-adjustment, the results suggest that institutional investors have a major problem if they limit their investments to stocks above a certain price level. Their odds of success deteriorate and remain low for stocks trading initially at $1 and above, reaching a negative MAR for stocks above $11. In the walk-forward optimization, I disregard any limit on initial price.

Conclusion

Have I run the risk of overoptimizing the parameters already and thus reduced the chances of finding a successful relative strength stock selection strategy? Not likely. The optimizations in this chapter have only eliminated those parameters that don't work. This is done to reduce the processing time in the final walk-forward optimizations that will find, if they exist, the best actual selection formula. Although many analysts use a standard optimization to find the best parameters, the best use of a standard optimization is to eliminate those parameters that will likely fail. If a set of parameters doesn't produce adequate results in the past, it very likely won't in the future. I have a better chance of finding a suitable set of parameters after I have eliminated those that have little chance of being profitable. Via the use of a sample of the database and the results from the standard optimizations of the seven principal variables, I have reduced computer processing time from multitrillion calculations to 13 million for each of nine walk-forward optimizations and kept the results within standard statistical bounds of confidence.

Endnotes

1. Levy, Robert A. "Relative Strength as a Criterion for Investment Selection." *Journal of Finance* 22, no. 4 (1967): 316–323.

2. Levy, Robert A. *The Relative Strength Concept of Common Stock Price Forecasting*. Larchmont, NY: Investors Intelligence, 1968.

4

Market Timing and
Walk-Forward Optimizing

This chapter looks at how to use walk-forward optimizing to find the parameters for any strategy system. Because the initial standard optimizations in Chapter 3, "Initial Standard Optimizations," show that large market declines have a significant adverse effect on relative strength stock selection, I reduce the effects of that observation by finding a suitable market-timing model that tells when the investor should be utilizing relative price strength and when he should be completely out of the market.

Market Timing

Control Indexes

Before devising a market-timing system, I must decide exactly what index to use in the timing. A buy-and-hold comparison to some index is one way to judge the results of any system, but the selection of which index to use is important because each acts differently than the other. The most common performance comparison is with the S&P 500. For portfolio work, however, this index has the major fault of being calculated using the market capitalization of each stock. Market capitalization is the product of the stock price times the amount of shares outstanding. Naturally, those stocks with many shares and a

high price have a larger influence on the index than do smaller companies with fewer shares. Investors do not allocate their portfolio
investments by capitalization. They allocate by position size, in most
cases attempting to make investment positions equal in value across
the portfolio. I thus discard the S&P 500 as a comparison index.

The Dow Jones Industrial is commonly quoted as a proxy for the
stock market in the news and public commentary, but it is also a poor
index to use for portfolio performance calculations because it weighs
its component stocks by price. A portfolio manager is not likely to
organize his portfolio based on the price of each holding. More likely,
he will organize the portfolio around equal dollar value positions.

The public index that most closely resembles the equal-dollar-
weighted index I use for determining each system's performance is
the Value Line Geometric Index. This index is calculated similarly to
my index, only with fewer stocks. Its behavior is considerably different from the S&P 500 because it weighs each stock equally by daily
percentage change. It is more similar to the way in which a portfolio is
constructed than the S&P or the Dow Jones. Its shortcoming is that it
represents only a fraction of the stocks traded on the U.S. exchanges.
To reduce this difficulty, I create an equal-dollar-weighted index from
the entire universe of 6,272 stocks in my database. Although you may
not be able to do this with your software, you can substitute the Value
Line Geometric Index in the final market-timing model and use the
same parameters. Figure 4.1 shows the index comparisons.

In Figure 4.1, note how differently the two indexes behave over
the same period. The database index had a greater return than the
S&P 500 and was less volatile. However, this lack of volatility makes
the timing of the market more difficult because there are no large,
easily identified swings as there are in the S&P 500.

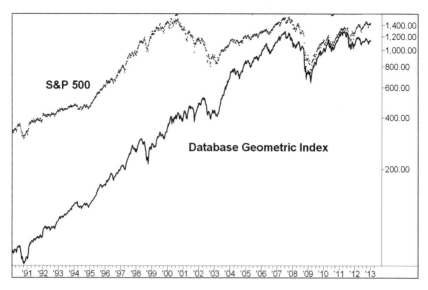

Figure 4.1 Comparison between the S&P 500 and my index of all stocks during the period January 1, 1990, through December 31, 2012.

Moving Averages

Many methods are used to determine when it is best to be invested in the stock market and when not to be. Most technical methods center on the use of moving averages.

A daily moving-average calculation finds the average daily price for a time sequence of prices and is plotted as a line on a price chart.

A moving average eliminates or reduces the magnitude of short-term fluctuations while portraying the longer-term trend. The result is a time sequence of smoother prices than the original. A *simple moving average*—the only kind I use—is the sum of the daily closing prices in the sequence divided by the number of prices in the sequence. Thus, a 25-day average has a total of all 25 prices divided by 25, the number of prices. This is called a 25-day average. When it is plotted each day, it is called a 25-day moving average. In Figure 4.2, you can see a chart of the price and moving average of the Value Line Geometric Index. It shows how often the price alone wiggles back and forth by itself and how the moving average converts those prices into a smooth line.

+VL:VLIC-I.TXT - Daily VL Geometric

Solid Line = 25-day moving average

'12 Feb Mar Apr May Jun Jul Aug Sep Oct Nov Dec '13

Figure 4.2   Value Line Geometric Index, January 1, 2012, through December 31, 2012, with a 25-day moving average.

There is only one controllable variable in a price moving average: the number of observations. As the number of observations increases, the time covered by the average increases in direct proportion, and the characteristics of the moving average change. The following visible alterations have been mathematically demonstrated:

1. A moving average of a certain length reduces cyclical fluctuations of the same length and less than or close to zero. Thus, a 25-day moving average reduces all fluctuations of 25 days or less to zero.

2. Because minor fluctuations are reduced to zero, major fluctuations of longer length are more obvious in the moving average. A 50-day cyclical fluctuation, for example, will be visible in a 25-day moving average, but a 5-day will not.

3. By controlling the moving-average length, cyclical fluctuations of certain lengths can thus be eliminated or emphasized in the data.

Moving-Average Crossover

Used alone, moving averages have a bad reputation as a timing mechanism because by their own nature, they are slow to react. If the market turns upward, a 25-day moving average will take roughly 12 days to turn up and confirm the new direction. This is both helpful and harmful. It is harmful because it is a late signal. It is helpful, however, because it will only turn up if the market upturn lasts longer than 12 days and the new trend is longer. For long-term investing, therefore, the length of a moving average can be important in eliminating short, false trend change signals.

One method analysts use to determine a new directional change in the market trend is a "change in slope" method that measures the slope of the moving average and records a signal when the slope accelerates or decelerates. Because a change in slope is not necessarily an indication of change in trend but may only signal a slowing in trend, measuring the slope gives early signals and many of them are false.

The use of a crossover, when the price crosses the moving average, is suggestive of a trend change. In Figure 4.2, you can see that when the trend changed, as represented by the moving average, the price had already crossed the moving average in the same direction as the trend change. However, you must also notice that not every crossover is a signal of trend change. There are many false crossovers, making the price crossover alone an unreliable indicator. However, when the price is again smoothed by a shorter moving average to eliminate the short fluctuations, the shorter-term moving-average crossover of the longer moving-average signals with more reliability and occurs less frequently. This method is called a *dual, moving-average-crossover system.*

A dual crossover system uses two moving averages: one called "fast" with a shorter time period and a "slow" average with a longer time period. The fast oscillates around the slow and gives signals when it crosses. A commonly used dual crossover system is called the *Golden Cross* and the *Death Cross*. The Golden Cross crossover, when the 50-day average crosses above the 200-day, confirms that a new, upward, intermediate-term price trend has occurred. The Death Cross, when the crossover is downward, confirms that the trend has turned downward. The reason for a 50-day average is that the crossover of the 200-day average makes fewer false signals than just a simple price crossover.

Studies show, however, that the parameters of 50 and 200 days don't produce reliable results. You can see in Figure 4.3 that the signals are so wrong that you would have performed better if you had acted oppositely from them during this period. The long-term history of the crossover is still valid but certainly not optimal. The time periods of 50 and 200 were derived in the days when price calculations were done on adding machines and 50 and 200 days sounded reasonable. Since then, many optimizations have shown that the actual periods to use differ with each market and are quite different than that earlier 50/200-day model.

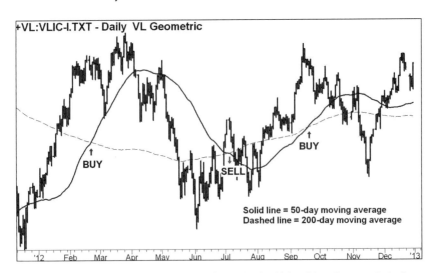

Figure 4.3   Golden Cross and Death Cross in the Value Line Geometric Index, January 1, 2012, through December 31, 2012.

In any moving-average crossover system, there are going to be false signals resulting from dull market periods when the fast average oscillates around the slow average. One way to reduce these false crossovers is the use of a *filter*. In a dual moving-average system, the filter is applied to the slow moving average and reduces the likelihood of a false crossover signal. Because minor fluctuations about the slow average are relatively constant in amplitude, the filter is calculated as a percentage slightly greater than the normal amplitude fluctuation. Thus when the shorter average breaks the filtered slow moving average, it suggests that the crossover is not one of the common minor oscillations but is instead a valid signal. This kind of crossover system is called a *filtered, dual, moving-average-crossover system*.

An alternate method to reduce false signals is to include an indicator of trend strength. The occurrence of false signals usually happens when the price action is trendless and the trend strength is weak. I prefer to use the ADX (Average Directional Movement Index) to determine trend strength. This indicator is described in more detail in the trading section of this book in Chapter 7, "Directional Movement Index (DMI) and the ADX." It determines from successive price changes the strength of those changes irrespective of direction. When it is rising, the trend strength is increasing. This is the desirable background for a moving-average crossover rather than when the ADX is declining and thus suggesting the trend strength is waning. The construction of the ADX is a little complicated, but importantly, it only requires one variable, the lookback period. A crossover system using a trend strength indicator is called a *trend-filtered, dual, moving-average-crossover system*.

The final adjustment to a moving-average system is to use two different systems, one for buys and one for sells. The reason for this is that in trading markets, the shape of price peaks and price troughs are completely different. A top is usually gradual and rounded, likely because greed, the major component of price advances, is slow to develop and slow to end. On the other hand, market lows tend to have very steep entries and sharp V-like reversals, likely because panic develops faster than greed. If one moving-average crossover system is optimized, it has to accommodate both types of price curves and is, thus, not as accurate as a moving-average system devoted to each. Thus, in my mind, the best moving-average market-timing system is a *double, trend-filtered, dual, moving-average-crossover system.* One moving-average-crossover system is optimized for buys and the other for sells.

Two final touches are added to the system. The first add-on is the use of a forward line (described in detail in Chapter 8, "Cycles and the Forward Line"). A forward line is another form of moving average that is plotted ahead of prices and provides a measure of the trend direction. When prices are above the forward line, the trend is upward, and conversely when it's below the line, the trend is downward. Like a moving average, its only variable is the length of the moving average, and it is always plotted half that length ahead of current prices. The reason for its use is that at times, a dual moving-average-crossover system will give a successful sell signal, but, because of the differences in moving-average lengths, a buy signal crossover may not occur. When this happens, the next upward price trend is missed. For this reason, I use a forward line to indicate if the trend is again upward and to generate a buy signal in that case. The forward line length is also part of the optimization.

The second add-on is a protective stop. This is a percentage of the entry price and is a point at which it is obvious that the buy signal was in error. It protects capital from false signals. This percentage is determined for the final system in a separate optimization after the moving-average parameters have been determined.

This moving-average-crossover system has six variables for which ideal parameters must be discovered. Each crossover portion requires a period for the fast and for the slow moving averages and a look-back period to be applied to the ADX calculation. In addition, a forward line length and eventually a protective stop percentage are also needed. Because it is easier to obtain, I use the Value Line Geometric Index as a proxy for the database equal-dollar-weighted index to find with walk-forward analysis the best-fit parameters for the final crossover system.

Walk-Forward Optimization and Analysis

Walk-forward optimization takes two major steps. The first is the optimization itself, and second is the analysis of the results.

Optimization

As discussed in Chapter 2, "Investment Strategies: Backtesting," walk-forward optimization uses an objective function as its goal and progresses through a time series of data leaving out portions that are not included in the optimization but are used instead to test the earlier optimization of parameters. The best way to proceed there is to follow the optimization of the dual, filtered, moving-average-crossover system for market timing of the Value Line Geometric Index.

The data used is available from Commodity Systems Inc. (www. csidata.com), namely daily closing prices of the Value Line Geometric Index from January 1985 through December 31, 2012. As mentioned earlier, this index is calculated similarly to the equal-dollar-weighted index used to discover parameters for the relative strength stock selection system in Chapter 5, "Stock Selection Using Relative Strength."

The *objective function*, the function by which I measure success or failure, is the MAR ratio, compound annual growth rate (CAGR) divided by the maximum drawdown (MDD) during the period optimized.

Following the TradeStation (www.tradestation.com) method of walk-forward optimization, the first step is to calculate the parameters that produce the highest level of MAR. In this optimization, the number of daily data points is 28 years (or 10,220 calendar days) over spans of 1 to 600 days for the six variables, four moving-average periods, and two ADX lookback periods. This amounts to a possible 4.665e+16 potential calculations. Rather than using a complete scan that looks at every one of the possible parameter combinations, I instead use a genetic algorithm that pretends the optimization is a breeding problem and progresses from generation to generation by culling out the lowest objective function results and keeping the best. This method saves considerable computer processing because once it eliminates a series of parameters as unworthy, it never uses them again, eventually focusing on the best fit to the MAR ratio in all the data and giving me about 90,000 possible parameter sets. These parameter sets are then run through the walk-forward optimization.

Standard optimization, as discussed in Chapter 2, tests whether a hypothetical system has merit by determining results over the entire test period. By finding positive results using a large number of parameters, it tells us if the system has a possibility of working in the future and eliminates parameters that are obviously irrelevant. In this way, standard optimization simplifies the eventual model study and reduces the number of parameters that will likely produce results. It does not give us a reliable system, however, because it does not adjust for the differences in market behavior that occurred during different stages of the study period nor does it tell us whether the results will be profitable in future markets. For that information, we need to use an optimization method that looks at short time periods sequentially to test the adaptability of the system to different market conditions and then tests these periodic results in new data not used in the optimization. The data used in each of these short optimizations is called the *in-sample* (IS) data, and the data used in the subsequent test is called the *out-of-sample* (OOS) data. Out-of-sample data is always kept separate from in-sample data; otherwise, the test would be contaminated by potential curve fitting and not be a true test of each optimization result.

The walk-forward optimization uses the standard optimization method of culling through the 90,000 preselected parameter sets to find the best fit for the period tested. For example, in a total test period of 10,000 days, it might take the first 1,000 days of in-sample data, determine through standard optimization the parameters that produce best fit to the objective function for that 1,000-day period, and then test that set of parameters over the next 500 days of out-of-sample data for results. The results should then be recorded for later analysis. The optimization then would slide forward in time to the 500th day for the second run, take the next 1,000 days for the standard optimization and test the results on the following 500 days of out-of-sample data. Figure 4.4 shows a simple graph of the process with only four runs. Notice that at no time within a run is the out-of-sample data used in its optimization. Again, the results of all out-of-sample tests are recorded for later use. This process continues through the entire data base. It overlaps the earlier data but at no time during any run is the out-of-sample data mixed with the in-sample data used in the run's optimization.

After the walk-forward optimization, the results from all of the out-of-sample tests are summarized in a table such as Table 4.1. The important measures of success are itemized and summarized for the eventual walk-forward analysis. Only those systems that pass each of the requirements are considered for further analysis.

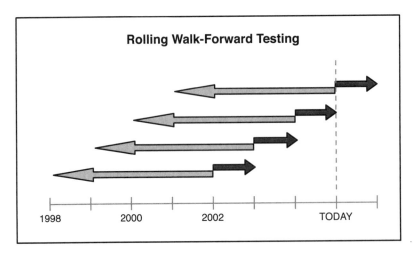

Source: www.TradingBlox.com.

Figure 4.4 Schematic of a rolling walk-forward optimization process. This is a process that "rolls" from data segment to data segment as opposed to an anchored walk-forward optimization that remains rooted with the initial data. Left-pointing bar = In-sample data standard optimization. Right-pointing bar = Out-of-sample test of parameters found in the earlier standard optimization. The statistics from each test are recorded for further analysis. At no time is the out-of-sample data (right-pointing arrow) used in the optimization data (left-pointing arrow) for each run. The results from each out-of-sample test are therefore a true measure in unknown data of the optimization.

Table 4.1 shows the five initial requirements for robustness in a system. The list is one of the results from a standard TradeStation summary showing a successful walk-forward optimization. The table heading shows this optimization's percent of the data that was out-of-sample (10%) and the number of successive runs (5) through the data. The criteria listed are as follows:

1. **Overall profitability**—The system is profitable in the out-of-sample tests.

2. **Walk-forward efficiency**—This is greater than 100%, meaning that the out-of-sample annualized return was greater than the in-sample return on an annualized basis. This is very positive because only a 50% performance is needed to project that the system will work in future data.

Table 4.1   Sample Results from One Walk-Forward Optimization That Passed the Basic Requirement for Robustness (initial analysis of a set of parameters derived from walk-forward optimization of a double, dual, filtered, moving-average-crossover system in the daily closes of the Value Line Geometric Index. Source: TradeStation)

Walk-Forward Analysis Results: OOS=10% WFRuns=5			
Symbol: +VLVLIC-I.TXT_ Daily			Strategy: Final Test
	Test Criteria	Result	Comment
1	Overall profitability	Pass	Total Profit > 0. System is likely to perform profitable on unseen data.
2	Walk-forward	Pass	Walk-Forward Efficiency >= 100%. System is likely to be successful at a future at a rate similar to those achieved during the optimization.
3	Consistency of	Pass	80%+ of walk-forward runs were profitable. System is likely to be successful in the future.
4	Distribution of	Pass	No individual time period contributed more than 70% of Total Net Profit.
5	Maximum	Pass	No individual run had a drawdown of more than 20% of cumulative equity at start of drawdown.
	OVERALL RESULT	PASS	Walk-Forward Efficiency >= 0%. System is likely to be successful in the future.

3. **Consistency**—At least 80% of the out-of-sample runs were profitable, meaning that profitability was not limited to just a few runs.

4. **Distribution**—No single run accounted for more than 70% of the total profit. This suggests that the profits were evenly distributed through the entire optimization through many market conditions, and were not due to one special run or set of circumstances.

5. **Maximum trade**—This is to measure the relation between a maximum trade and all other trades in a run. It is used to prevent a system from having one large profitable trade that outweighs all the others, disproportionally influencing the profit results, but may be an anomaly.

In the market-timing optimizations, at least four systems met the basic requirements for a robust system. Once these "finalists" are determined, I make further calculations to analyze their potential and to determine the best one for the market-timing model. These systems are shown in Table 4.2 with additional statistics.

Table 4.2   Summary Results for the Four Market-Timing Systems in the Value Line Geometric Index to Have Passed the Basic Requirements for a Robust System That Will Have Better-Than-Average Results in the Future

		Value Line Geometric Daily January 1, 1985–December 31, 2012			
		Optimization Statistics			
	System Number	**1**	**2**	**3**	**4**
1	RUNS	5	5	10	10
2	OOS%	10%	15%	20%	25%
		Parameters for Variables			
3	Buy Fast SMA	6	8	4	6
4	Buy Slow SMA	28	20	28	28
5	Buy ADX Lookback	6	6	6	6
6	Sell Fast SMA	15	15	15	5
7	Sell Slow SMA	51	51	51	31
8	Sell ADX Lookback	5	5	5	36
9	Forward Line Length	15	18	17	15
		Out-of-Sample Results			
10	Initial Capital	$100,000	$100,000	$100,000	$100,000
11	OOS Ann NP$	$11,721	$7,985	$7,763	$9,881
12	OOS CAGR	10.73%	10.26%	10.43%	12.10%
13	OOS #Trades	34	35	36	45
14	OOS Trades Prftbl	61.76%	60.00%	55.56%	55.56%

		Value Line Geometric Daily January 1, 1985–December 31, 2012			
		Optimization Statistics			
	System Number	1	2	3	4
15	OOS MDD %	35.95%	31.55%	27.85%	25.26%
16	%Profitable Runs	80%	80%	80%	80%
17	Profit Factor	5.05	4.32	4.68	4.31
18	MAR	0.30	0.33	0.37	0.48
19	WFE	130.55%	74.78%	67.43%	66.65%

In rows 1 through 2, the testing parameters are noted. Each system is the result of a different combination of runs and percentage of data set aside as out-of-sample for testing of each run's standard optimization. Generally, in systems that have few trades, a large number of runs produces only a few trades per run, perhaps even no trades per run, and thus ends with many inconclusive trade statistics. In optimizations such as the market-timing problem, because I can expect relatively few trades, I suspect that the most trustworthy results will come from optimizations with only 5 to 10 runs.

In rows 3 through 9 are the final parameters suggested by each model's walk-forward optimization for use in the future. They are each labeled in the left column. Below the parameter section are further test results. These are calculations made on the total out-of-sample results of each optimization.

Further statistics by row in Table 4.2 are as follows:

10. *Initial Capital* at $100,000 is the same for all optimizations. It is the hypothetical value of the system at its beginning of the optimization.

11. *OOS Ann NP$* is the annualized net profit in dollars for the system in the out-of-sample data. It is used for comparison between each system to show which was ultimately the most profitable. It does not include the risk assumed in the system but just the profits. The most profitable system was #1.

12. *OOS CAGR* is the annual compound annual return for the system in the out-of-sample data. It is the numerator in the MAR ratio below in row 15. This is one of the most important figures in assessing the value of a specific system formula for future use. System #4 has the highest CAGR.

13. *OOS #Trades* is the number of trades generated by the system in the out-of-sample data. For statistical reliance, 30 trades as a minimum should occur. All of the systems had this figure.

14. *OOS Trades Prftbl* stands for the percentage of all trades in the out-of-sample data that were profitable. The percentage of profitable trades is important in moving-average-crossover systems where the system usually incurs small losses until one large trend is identified. The higher the profitable percentage of trades, the less risk of a major drawdown. System #1 has the highest percentage of profitable trades.

15. *OOS MDD%* is the percentage maximum drawdown in all the out-of-sample data. All systems show a maximum drawdown less than my usual threshold of 20%. System #4 has the lowest maximum drawdown percentage.

16. *%Profitable Runs* is the percentage of all out-of-sample runs that are profitable. The higher the percentage, the better the system has worked in different market conditions and thus the more likely it will adjust to and be successful in future market conditions. The standard cutoff is 50%, and 80% to 100% demonstrates the highest level of robustness in a system. All four systems were 80%.

17. *Profit Factor* is the ratio of total gross profit divided by total gross loss. It should be above 1.00, otherwise the system loses money. System #1 had the highest Profit Factor.

18. *MAR* is the ratio of the system annualized net profit to its maximum dollar drawdown. It is the objective function for all my optimizations. The MAR ratio in system #4 is the highest due to its high return and small maximum drawdown.

19. *WFE* stands for walk-forward efficiency and is the ratio of the annualized net profit for out-of-sample data to the annualized net profit in-sample data. It is the most important of all result measurements because it quantifies just how successful

the derived system has performed in out-of-sample data. The rule of thumb is that in the future, the system will perform at least as well as half the WFE. A WFE greater than 100% is considered superb. System #1 is the system with the highest WFE at 130.55%.

To determine the best of all systems, I look primarily at two factors: the walk-forward efficiency rating (WFE) and the MAR. The MAR is the objective function and thus has the higher weighting. Of the systems in Table 4.2, #1 and #4 stand out as the best. At this point, because one has the higher MAR and the other the higher WFE, I first perform a walk-forward optimization for a protective stop and will decide on the final market timing model based on those results.

Protective Stop

Because the final models include an estimated maximum drawdown of between 25% and 35%, I optimize each for a percentage protective stop. This optimization arrived at the figures in Table 4.3. There is no question that system #4 comes out on top. It outperformed system #1 in every category once an optimized protective stop was added.

Table 4.3 Summary of the Two Best Trend-Adjusted, Dual, Moving-Average-Crossover Systems for the Value Line Geometric Index from January 1, 1985 Through December 31, 2012 When Adjusted for an Optimized Percentage Protective Stop

	System #1	System #4
Percent Protective Stop	5.67%	8.87%
Net Profit	$238,761	$448,772
CAGR	10.56%	15.42%
Maximum Trade Drawdown	11.96%	8.57%
MAR	0.97	1.80
WFE	99.94%	175.13%

For comparison, the buy-and-hold CAGR for the Value Line Geometric Index over the same period is 3.19% with a maximum drawdown of 69.8%. By using the percentage protective stop in system #4, the maximum drawdown for the system declines to 8.57% from 25.26%, but the percentage of profitable trades also declines slightly to 51.43% from 55.56% as more of them are closed from the stop. In addition, the CAGR increases because the poor trades are eliminated early to 15.42%, the MAR rises considerably above the ideal of 1.00, and the WFE is far above the desired 1.00. All in all, the protective stops have provided a remarkable improvement to an already profitable system.

Conclusion

You have seen how I develop an investment market-timing system using walk-forward optimization. The parameters must be reoptimized periodically to adjust for any changes in market character since the original study. This market-timing system will be integrated into the selection system to be addressed in Chapter 5. Its purpose is to give signals to the selection system as to when the overall stock market looks weak or strong. It is intended to reduce the large drawdowns that have occurred in both the ranking and raw-ratio models by signaling when the stock selection index should cease purchasing new stock and liquidate its entire holdings in preparation for a general market decline. It thus should smooth the equity curve for the selection system, improve the CAGR, and reduce the oscillations about its upward trend.

5

Stock Selection Using Relative Strength

During almost my entire investment career, I have considered that the best way to select stocks for investment or trading is through a relative strength method. By *relative strength,* I mean the strength of a stock's price over a specified time compared with that of other stocks. All studies that I have seen from academia and professional investment management journals and books have substantiated this method as the one consistent method of beating the odds in Wall Street. There is no question that it works. The question then is how you calculate relative strength to capitalize on the inherent ability for strong stocks to continue with their strength for enough time to provide a profit to the investor. The classic Levy method I have always used is the ratio of the closing price to a 26-week moving average of those prices, ranked against the same ratio for all other stocks. My original work was to quantify and optimize the best rank for purchase and sale of the stock. That was the subject of my first book on beating the market. It now turns out that with more modern optimization methods at my disposal, the earlier method can be improved upon.

Review and Present Standing

Let me first review where I am in this stock selection study. The analysis to this point has been predominately through standard optimization. This method has its obvious flaws in that it tells me nothing about how a derived model will perform in the future. What it does tell me, however, is what does *not* contribute to performance. It eliminates from consideration not only variables but also parameters for variables that seem to have no value. From the factors that remain after those that failed are discarded, the next step is to perform walk-forward optimizations on the remaining variables and their most likely parameters. From analysis of those results, I have a viable model that should reliably profit in the future.

So far, the best ranking system derived in Chapter 2, "Investment Strategies: Backtesting," using standard optimization, has a 196-day lookback, a 97% relative strength rank for buys, and a 59% rank for sales. This is slightly different from my original formula of 182 days, 97%, and 52%. However, it is the ideal because it produces the best result in the standard optimization. It is not the final formula, however. What it tells me is the level of MAR, compound annual growth rate (CAGR), and maximum drawdown (MDD) that I should strive to match in the walk-forward optimization. It is not likely that a derived, robust system will outperform a curve-fitted system from a standard optimization. There is a slight chance that walk-forward optimizing can produce a slightly better model by adjusting during the shorter optimization spans to the vagaries of the markets at those times, but the overall results will not likely exceed the ideal obtained from the standard optimization.

In addition to the curve-fitted system, the walk-forward optimization must outperform the long-term buying-and-holding all stocks in the database as well. This represents what the investor could have performed by avoiding any system and just buying a representative sample of the database on January 1, 1990, and holding it until December 12, 2012. Table 5.1 shows the performance statistics of the three methods available so far that must be at least matched by the walk-forward optimization.

The highest threshold to achieve is the one derived from the curve-fit standard optimization in Chapter 3, "Initial Standard Optimizations." To develop a system that matches or is superior is the present challenge. The old method of 26 weeks, 97 buy rank, and 52 sell rank is still the superior working system that has been tested over time in actual use.

Table 5.1 Comparative Performance Statistics of the Buy-and-Hold System and the Standard Optimized System

	Standard Optimization (Ideal Solution)	Buy-and-Hold	Old Method from Earlier Book
Compound Annual Growth Rate (CAGR)	22.58%	3.76%	19.45%
Maximum Drawdown (MDD)	62.0%	49.5%	62.3%
MAR (CAGR to MDD)	.36	.076	.31

Considerations not included in these systems but integrated into the walk-forward optimization are percentage stops, initial volume, initial price, and a market-timing model that was discussed in Chapter 4, "Market Timing and Walk-Forward Optimizing." The testing under standard optimization produces no advantage from the use of percentage stops or initial price. They are thus discarded from further consideration. Their results were interesting from a theoretical standpoint but useless for the ideal relative strength stock selection model. The remaining variable that did produce favorable results was initial volume. The 50-day moving average of volume above 10,000 shares produced a large jump in the performance measurements. Because its 10,000 share level maintained the same performance for higher levels of volume, there is no need to optimize it further, and it is included in the walk-forward optimization as a constant.

An Alternate, Simpler Selection Method

I have found, to my amazement, in performing walk-forward optimizations on the three basic parameters for the standard ranking method calculation that the ranking is not necessary. The raw ratio of closing price to a moving average works almost as well as the ranking system. It is so much simpler for the average investor to calculate. Rather than sort through thousands of results to arrive at a ranking figure, the individual need only use a spreadsheet to calculate the necessary ratio and determine whether a stock is a buy, sell, or hold.

The principal difficulty with ranking, aside from the enormous amount of data and processing it requires, is that the results select stocks with the same relative criteria in all markets whether advancing or declining. This means that the highest-ranked stocks in a declining market are selected for addition to a portfolio even though they themselves may be declining in price but just at a lesser rate than other stocks. The problem of buying strong stocks just before a market decline can be partially mitigated by a market-timing method that signals when not to be in the market at all. But the risk of capital loss is still great in a portfolio loaded with stocks just before a market decline. The traditional method of protecting against loss in portfolio positions is having protective and trailing sell stops, of course, for each stock. Having tested protective stops in a standard optimization, I find that they do not work well in limiting maximum drawdown. The reason is that when a stock is eliminated from a portfolio, the normal reaction is to replace it with another stock that meets the buy criteria. With a relative strength system at the beginning of a market decline, this means the portfolio manager is buying stocks at the worst time.

The age-old problem for portfolio managers is what to do with the cash received from a stock sold on a sale. How do you know if the money should be kept aside, especially when you see many stocks being "stopped out" of a portfolio? Should it be reinvested in new stocks that meet the relative strength buy-rank level? The answer, surprisingly, is using a straight ratio of closing price to a moving average. In this method, the strong stocks are always chosen, thus satisfying the widely accepted and tested theory that strong stocks remain strong, but the ranking is disregarded. What will happen during the normal market cycle is that as the market advances, more stocks will meet the ratio level for a buy, and as the market peaks, the number of stocks with that superior strength will decline, thus limiting the selection list to fewer potential stocks as well as warn that the market is slowing its advance. Chartcraft, Inc., (www.investorsintelligence.com) for many years has calculated the number of stocks above their 10- and 30-week moving averages and used this figure as a market-timing device when it changes direction. Using the raw ratio alone, unranked, avoids the problem of investing in stocks that are stronger than other stocks but are not especially attractive as investments.

The additional beauty of such a system is that it is simple to calculate. All that is needed is the correct buy and sell ratios and the period for the moving average. Anyone with a spreadsheet can determine from these calculations whether a particular stock is a buy, hold, or sell, without having to resort to the complex calculations necessary to calculate the ratios for thousands of stocks and rank them in order of their ratio. Just the ratio itself is needed.

The Walk-Forward Optimizations

Despite the arguments for either the raw-ratio method or the ranking method, each must first be tested for optimal parameters and in the process for robustness (probability of continuing in the future). As mentioned ad nauseam throughout this book, I prefer the walk-forward method of optimization for such a determination. Without resorting to waiting for future results to prove or disprove a set of parameters, the walk-forward method simulates the future by using data not included in each optimization and also calculates a series of optimizations that realistically simulates the real world where systems must adjust to changing market character. The following is the summary of the walk-forward optimizations for both the ranking system and the raw-ratio system.

Ranking System

Walk-forward optimizations looking for the most robust ranking system settle on three possibilities. These models all include the 10,000 share volume constraint as well as the basic three variables of lookback period, buy rank, and sell rank. They do not include the market-timing model from Chapter 4. The three most robust systems for the ranking system are shown in Table 5.2.

Table 5.2   Final Walk-Forward Optimization Results for the Relative Strength Ranking System

Walk-Forward Optimization and Analysis Relative Strength Rank Stock Selection Models 1,002 stocks for the period 1/1/1990–12/31/12			
ID Number	**1**	**2**	**3**
RUNS	5	20	20	
OOS%	30%	20%	30%	
IS	2673	1400	878	
OS	1146	350	376	
Lookback	175	182	210	Lookback
Buy Rank	98	97.5	97	RS Buy
Sell Rank	59	58	58	RS Sell
Out-of-Sample Test Results			
Initial Capital	100,000	100,000	100,000	Standards
Ann NP$	$384,224	$581,202	$733,563	
# Trades/Ann	76	68	63	s/b >30
%CAGR	30.93%	28.94%	28.40%	s/b > 20%
%MDD	57.76%	54.72%	56.02%	s/b <20%
Largest Prft Run%	41%	74%	37%	s/b < 50%
%Runs Profitable	100%	70%	80%	s/b > 50%
Sharpe	0.96	0.78	0.89	s/b > .80
MAR	0.54	0.48	0.49	s/b > .50
R-squared	0.90	0.83	0.87	s/b > .80
WFE	2.58	8.6	13.79	s/b >1.00

Table 5.2 is similar to earlier tables and shows the parameters for the models as well as the desired levels of test results to demonstrate robustness and reliability for the future. Those desired levels are as follows:

- **Ann NP$**—Stands for the annualized net profit in the out-of-sample results. Larger is better. This is the figure that is divided by the annual net profit of the in-sample optimization results to determine the walk-forward efficiency ratio (WFE).

- **# Trades/Ann**—Stands for the number of trades in the out-of-sample results per year. It should be greater than 30. All systems meet this requirement.

- **%CAGR**—Stands for the compound annual growth rate, or rate of return, for the out-of-sample model when linked through all runs in the optimization. To match the standard optimization results, this figure should be 22.6%. Each of the models exceeds this rate of return with System #2 exceeding 30%.

- **%MDD**—Stands for the maximum drawdown during all out-of-sample runs. My preference is for an MDD less than 20%. When studying individual stock behavior, I can meet this objective easily with protective stops. As Chapter 3 shows, however, protective stops in individual stocks have little effect, if any, on a portfolio of stocks. The drawdowns in this study are due to the general market corrections, not on the selection system. The market-timing model created in Chapter 4 is an attempt to close down the system when the evidence suggests a large decline. The result for the addition of the market-timing model to the most robust system is discussed later in this chapter.

- **Largest Prft Run%**—Stands for the largest single profitable run percentage return. It is important that no one run account for a majority of the out-of-sample performance because it could be an anomaly and also suggests that the final results are due to only one trade. The standard is for the largest profitable run to account for less than 50% of the total profit. System #3 is the only system to meet that requirement.

- **%Runs Profitable**—Stands for the percent of all runs in the optimization that were profitable. A high percentage is desirable because it suggests that the model is effective in different market conditions. The standard is 50%, but I prefer 80% or better. All the systems were at 65% or better.

- **Sharpe**—Stands for the Sharpe ratio, a ratio of adjusted return versus volatility that is popular among portfolio managers and theorists. I do not set much value to it because it considers volatility to be a risk measurement, which it is not. In this study, where short sales are not considered, it has more value as a comparative measure.

- **MAR**—Stands for the ratio of CAGR to MDD, the annual growth rate to the maximum drawdown. A ratio greater than 1.0 is excellent and above 0.50 is satisfactory. In this optimization, all models are adversely affected equally by the large maximum drawdowns from market corrections, yet two of the three were greater than the 0.50 requirement, and the third was very close.

- **R-squared**—Shows the level of correlation that the equity curve in the out-of-sample results have to a straight line from opening to closing. It gives an idea of how well the results are steady and not subject to corrections. The highest possible with a perfect correlation to a straight line would be 1.00. No correlation would be 0.0. The minimum level for robustness is 0.70. All the systems exceeded this level.

- **WFE**—Stands for the walk-forward efficiency ratio, the most important statistic in this table. The ratio is calculated by dividing the out-of-sample annualized rate of return (CAGR) by the in-sample annualized rate of return. It measures the ability of the out-of-sample tests to duplicate the in-sample optimizations. A reading above 0.50 is considered robust; above 1 is superb.

Note

Analysts use other ratios to determine if the maximum drawdown is an outlier from all other drawdowns or something to frequently expect. I do not use them in this analysis because the maximum drawdown is due mostly to market conditions and is beyond the selection system's ability to correct.

I select system #3 as the most robust of the ranking systems. It has the lowest maximum drawdown, the lowest portion of its profits attributable to one trade, the highest percent of runs profitable in the optimization results, and the highest walk-forward efficiency ratio (WFE).

Raw System

Performing the same analysis on the ratio alone without ranking, I find the optimizations not quite as favorable as for the ranking system but still ahead of the standard optimization baseline in performance and certainly calculated more easily. This makes the raw ratio system an excellent technique for individuals to use in selecting stocks for their private portfolios. A subscription to an expensive service that calculates the ratios and ranks is unnecessary, and the results are still above the mainstream average performance. Table 5.3 shows the four best raw-ratio systems found through walk-forward optimization and some of their statistics.

Table 5.3   Final Walk-Forward Optimization Results for the Raw-Ratio System

	Walk-Forward Optimization and Analysis Relative Strength Price Ratio Stock Selection Models 1,002 stocks for the period 1/1/1990–12/31/12				
ID Number	**1**	**2**	**3**	**4**	
RUNS	10	10	20	20	
OOS%	20%	30%	20%	30%	
IS	2400	1589	1400	878	
OS	600	681	350	376	
Lookback	406	406	413	427	Lookback
Buy Ratio	1.42	1.41	1.47	1.47	RS Buy
Sell Ratio	1.04	1.04	1.03	1.04	RS Sell
	Out-of-Sample Test Results				
Initial Capital	**100,000**	**100,000**	**100,000**	**100,000**	**Standards**
Ann NP$	217,355	405,235	362,504	389,290	
# Trades/Ann	117	110	93	88	s/b >30
%CAGR	24.54%	26.21%	24.84%	23.80%	s/b > 20%
%MDD	47.87%	53.61%	47.28%	52.89%	s/b <20%
Largest Prft Run%	38%	53%	33%	28%	s/b < 50%
% Runs Profitable	90%	80%	80%	85%	s/b > 50%
Sharpe	0.82	0.91	0.86	0.85	s/b > .80
MAR	0.46	0.49	0.46	0.40	s/b > .50
R-squared	0.92	0.91	0.89	0.85	s/b > .80
WFE	7.02	7.95	7.42	10.93	s/b >1.00

I select system #4 as the most robust of the raw-ratio systems discovered in the walk-forward optimization. All four systems have merit.
This is the formula that individuals should use to select stocks without
going through the trouble and expense of calculating the ranks of all
stocks. The only difference to account for my selection is that #4 has
the highest WFE. In addition, its number of trades is small, suggesting that profits are made with less trading, and its largest profitable
run is low, suggesting that it is not being dominated by one period

of time or one trade. But aside from the WFE, these differences are minor. Any of the four should work in the future.

The ranking system adds value to the relative strength method. The use of just the ratio, without ranking it against all other stocks, provides similar results. Table 5.4 shows a comparison in vital statistics between the two methods. The differences are significant, but both are well ahead of most other investment methods. The annual rate of return for the ranking system's best system is 28.4% versus 23.8% for the best of the raw ratio systems. Have you done as well in your investments? For those seeking an easily calculated system for selecting stocks for a portfolio, the difference is not worth the time and trouble of calculating the ratio for all stocks and then sorting them in the order of their strength. For someone with just a few stocks of interest, to calculate the ratio of the closing price to the 427 calendar-day (61-week) moving average is easy. The buy and sell decision is equally as easy. Just buy the stock when its ratio advances above 1.47, and sell it when the ratio declines below 1.04.

Table 5.4 Final Walk-Forward Optimization Results for the Relative Strength Systems—Ranking and Raw Ratio—Including the Use of a 10,000 Share Limit for Purchase

Walk-Forward Optimization and Analysis Comparison Between Ranking System and Raw Ratio System Relative Strength Stock Selection 1,002 stocks for the period 1/1/1990–12/31/12			
System	Ranking	Raw Ratio	
RUNS	20	20	
OOS%	30%	30%	
IS	1589	1589	
OS	681	681	
Lookback	211	428	Lookback
Buy Ratio	97	147	RS Buy
Sell Ratio	58	104	RS Sell

Walk-Forward Optimization and Analysis
Comparison Between Ranking System and Raw Ratio System
Relative Strength Stock Selection
1,002 stocks for the period 1/1/1990–12/31/12

System	Ranking	Raw Ratio	
	Out-of-Sample Test Results		
Initial Capital	100,000	100,000	Standards
Ann NP$	733,563	389,290	
# Trades	63	88	s/b >30
%CAGR	28.40%	23.80%	s/b > 20%
%MDD	56.02%	52.89%	s/b <20%
Largest Pft Run%	37%	28%	s/b < 50%
%Runs Profitable	80%	85%	s/b > 50%
Sharpe	0.89	0.85	s/b > .80
MAR	0.49	0.40	s/b > .50
R-squared	0.87	0.85	s/b > .80
WFE	13.79	10.93	s/b >1.00
# Standards Met	8	8	

Addition of Market Timing System

When I add the market-timing model derived in Chapter 4, the performance results improve because the portfolio is not burdened by the very large drawdowns that occurred in the years 2000 through 2009. Figure 5.1 shows a graphic of the performance of the ranking system adjusted for market timing, the ranking system by itself, the equal-dollar-weighted stock index, the Value Line Geometric Index, and the Standard & Poor's 500 Index.

I add the S&P Index because it commonly is used in the comparison of mutual fund and other portfolio performance. The chart shows what a lousy index it is for performance comparisons. Both it and the Value Line are comprised of large capitalization stocks. I use the Value Line in the market timing because it is constructed similar to the equal-dollar-weighted stock index I use for comparison, but both indexes fall far behind in overall price performance. The equal-dollar-weighted index is representative of the percentage change of all stocks, not just the large ones. As the earlier standard optimization (Chapter 3) on price as an initial selection criteria show, the lower the price, the better the performance. With these lower price stocks included in the equal-dollar-weighted stock market index, the performance of the index, of course, has been stronger than the more popular indexes that represent only larger stocks. The equal-dollar-weighted index is a better proxy of the entire stock market because it includes the percentage change of all individual issues and thus reflects what all stock investments have done. It is a difficult index to beat, and this is likely why it is not used in the portfolio management business.

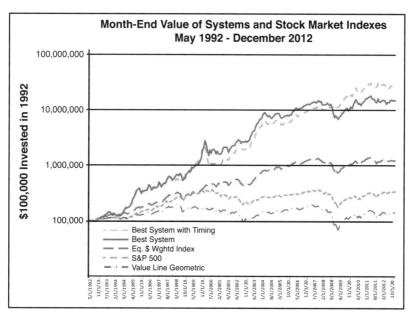

Figure 5.1 Month-end values of the best relative strength ranking system, the same system adjusted for market timing, the equal-dollar-weighted stock index of the stock universe used in this study, the Value Line Geometric Index, and the Standard & Poor's 500 Index, for the period May 28, 1992 (when the first relative strength signal was given) until December 31, 2012.

Conclusion

At the beginning of this book, I outlined my intention to improve the relative price strength system earlier devised. That has been accomplished. Where the old method generated an annual return of 19.45% and a maximum drawdown of 62.3%, the new system generates a return close to 30% per year but still a high drawdown at 52.89%. Market timing can reduce that maximum drawdown and increase return to near 35% per year. What I had not intended but am pleasantly surprised by is the fact that favorable results also can be achieved without resorting to the tedious calculating and sorting required for the ranking system. Excellent performance results can be obtained by using the raw ratio and its derived parameters for buying and selling.

6

Trading Strategies

I read somewhere that the average working life span of a stock investor is 16–17 years. That is 17 years from his first year as a professional investor to when he retires, gets promoted to management, or busts out. It occurred to me when I read this that the market itself changes character every 16–17 years as well. It travels in long upward trends for 16–17 years and then changes to a generally flat trend with very wide oscillations. For example, the market began a long upward trend in the mid-1980s that ended in 2000. Since then, the market has been generally flat with oscillations in 2003 and 2008 of 60% or more. Figure 6.1 shows these changes in character over the 90 years between 1920 and 2010. I point this out to show that the stock market is dynamic, as we all know, but exists in only two basic modes—steady upward trending or sideways trending with large oscillations every 16–17 years. Perhaps this is due to the working life span of investors or the working life span of investors is due to the inherent change in the market. I suspect the latter because the different modes require different investment strategies and thus will bust out the investment manager who cannot adjust. Upward trends require a buy-and-hold strategy that trades very little and just holds investments "for the long term." The oscillating market with no discernible trend requires a market-timing strategy to avoid the large intervening corrections that wipe out investments for several years. The last few years, since 2000, have been years when a market-timing strategy would have been successful especially because the latter correction in the market was more than 60%, a decline that takes a lot of subsequent advances to recover from. Thus, market oscillations in the oscillating period tend to ruin the buy-and-hold trend investors, and the long upward trend discredits the market-timing types who often sell their positions much too soon, every 16–17 years.

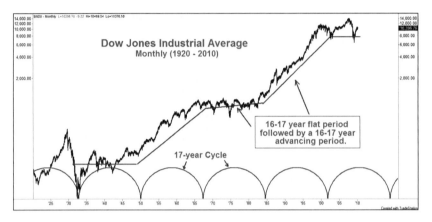

Created with TradeStation. © TradeStation Technologies, Inc. All rights reserved.

Source: Kirkpatrick, Charles, and Julie Dahlquist. *Technical Analysis*. 2nd ed. Upper Saddle River, NJ: FT Press, 2012.

Figure 6.1 16–17 year change in stock market trend from 1920 through 2010.

This behavior is the basis for classical technical analysis that argues for prices to travel in trends with periodic intervals of consolidation. Consolidations form patterns that the technician attempts to interpret for an indication pointing which way the market will "break out" of the pattern and continue in another trend. These formations have often been referred to as *continuation* or *reversal* patterns, but recent evidence from more rigorous tests of patterns has shown that most patterns do not exhibit a tendency in either direction. The designation of continuation and reversal pattern, therefore, is inaccurate.

This dynamic change in market behavior is not limited to 16-year cycles, however. It occurs over much shorter periods from weekly data to minute-by-minute data. To trade a market over shorter periods, the trader must be adept at recognizing when the market characteristic has changed and change his trading method accordingly. Traditionally, the two trading methods for the two types of market mode are the *trend* trading method and the *reversion-to-mean* trading method. Both can work in both types of markets once certain adjustments are made.

Trend trading means that the trader looks for patterns or uses indicators such as moving averages to discover when a trend is beginning in a particular stock or market and jumps on the trend as soon as he or she is satisfied that it fulfills the requirements for a trend that will last for a long time. A trend trader usually holds a position until the signs appear that the trend is ending. This method has no price target at which the position will be exited. Comparatively, the reversion-to-mean trader trades the oscillations around a trend. As long as the trend is steady, flat, or otherwise, and the oscillations about it have well-defined upper and lower bounds, the trader will have targets at those upper and lower bounds of the oscillations. A reversion-to-mean trader could buy, for example, a stock at the lower bound of a series of oscillations with the intention of selling the stock at the upper bound of the next oscillation. It means he anticipates a low to occur within a range of prices that have occurred in previous deviations from the trend and intends to sell when the price reaches the "normal" upward deviation. He is not trading the trend direction but only the deviations from that trend on the assumption that the price will continue to oscillate in a predictable manner. In some cases, the target is the mean itself. When I describe the forward line in Chapter 8, "Cycles and the Forward Line," you will see how prices tend to stabilize at certain predefined levels.

Each of these shorter advances and declines are small trends in themselves, and can be treated as such by the trend trader by adjusting his *period of interest*. By periods of interest, I mean a trader's ideal and preferred trade time horizon. Traders look at price bars (high, low, open, close) at various time intervals—some at 5-minute price bars, for example, others at daily bars, others at 20-minute bars.

There are an infinite number of periods over which to trade trends or oscillations, mostly determined by the trader's ability and preference in trading. The trader can watch his securities once a day or sit at a terminal all day, trading minor oscillations. Every trader determines his period of interest based on personality, time available for trading, hardware, software, and ability. When a market transitions from one mode to another, the trader can adjust by changing either his period of interest or his trading method. Figure 6.2 shows an example of this.

Figure 6.2   Dow Jones Industrial weekly, showing oscillating market, and Dow Jones Industrial daily, showing trending market with a different period of interest.

A trend trader who uses only trend-trading methods and is having difficulty in a trendless market can conform to market mode change by adjusting his period of interest, as in this example, from weekly bars to hourly bars. Conversely, the reversion-to-mean trader can adjust when a market mode changes to a long upward trend to trading the ups and downs within the trend or within corrective periods of the trend. Here, I show an oscillating market on a weekly basis, but a trending market when the period of interest is changed from weekly to hourly.

I prefer trend trading to reversion-to-mean trading. The choice is personal. I know successful traders who use either and sometimes both methods successfully. Most trading models I use assume a trend once recognized will continue until it reverses. Most trend traders look for consolidation patterns and act when the price breaks out of a pattern. This is called a *breakout* strategy and when combined with leverage and money management can be very profitable. Another trend-trading system is the use of moving averages as I use them for market timing in the investment section of this book. Rather than popular conventional methods like moving-average crossover systems for trading, however, I use a variation of the breakout method that first looks for indications of an existing trend coming to an end. The end of a trend is the time when the mode changes from trend to oscillations. It is a period that is preparatory to another trend and is, thus, the first warning that a new trend may begin soon. In trend trading, the object is to get into the trend right at the beginning. The trade-off in this method is that often the indications of the beginning of a trend are false and the trend never develops or, worse, develops in the wrong direction than anticipated. Some traders will wait for proof that a trend has indeed begun, but they lose the early stage of the trend, which is often the most profitable. It is the price they pay for surety. They will often wait for a trend to begin and jump on the trend when it suffers a short setback, thus integrating a trend method with a reversion-to-mean strategy but depending on the trend for the profit and the reversion for the actual entry into the trade. Rather than waiting for such proof and waiting for setback to enter a position, I prefer to use indicators other than just price to confirm the existence of a new trend. The first of these is the indicator to tell me that the previous trend is over. By using this indicator, I know that I will not be sucked into the trading crowd that has been playing that old trend. I also know that eventually a new trend will begin at some time, and I want to be participating in it. That new trend will require certain indicators to fall into line, and my confidence in its existence is bolstered by the favorable indicator evidence. For a trader, unlike an investor, the actual direction of the trend is irrelevant because money can be made on a long trade as well as on a short trade. Thus, my trading systems have no directional bias but just look for the beginning of a directional price move in either direction.

A *short trade* is made when the stock is borrowed and sold and later purchased back at a lower price. The profit in the trade comes from the difference between what was paid for the stock versus what it was earlier sold for. In the futures markets, a short sale is really not a short sale in the same vein as in the stock market.

Also different from the investor, the trader usually doesn't look at the entire market but instead picks certain securities, stocks, or futures to trade based on their liquidity and volatility. As mentioned in the investment section of this book, the preferred trading vehicle is also a volatile stock.

Using measures of volatility and liquidity, defined by rapid price changes and active trading volume, the trader selects issues to trade and limits them to a small enough number that they can be monitored closely. With computers, that process is made easier, and traders now have the ability to watch many more issues than they could when I first started. My preference for issues is the list that is derived in the investment section of stocks that have high relative price strength. I know these stocks have a tendency toward traveling in trends and have liquidity and volatility. The difference between trading them and investing in them, however, is the difference in period of interest. The investment method depends on weekly price data, whereas my trading depends on hourly price data. These are the trends I want to take advantage of.

What follows in the next chapters is a description of the methods I use. I first cover three indicator calculations—the Directional Movement Index (DMI), its derivative, the Average Directional Movement Index (ADX), and the forward line (FWL)—the rationale behind their use, the combined method, and some models derived from this method. As examples, I optimize simple systems using an Exchange Traded Fund (ETF) with high liquidity, broad capitalization base, and sufficient volatility. The methods are applicable to any stock, commodity, or liquid, freely traded security, but I warn that before you act, you first experiment with different parameters in the models because each security has its own personality that requires its own set of parameters. The ETF I show is the SSO (ProShares Ultra S&P 500). It has a history long enough to provide statistically relevant results in walk-forward analysis.

7

Directional Movement Index (DMI) and the ADX

The Genius of J. Welles Wilder, Jr.

In 1978, J. Welles Wilder wrote a book called *New Concepts in Technical Trading Systems*,[1] which is, in my mind, one of the best books ever written about systems and indicators for the stock market (and any other market). The book introduces indicators never considered before, yet they are used today by many traders who have never known their origin. Indicators like the Relative Strength Index (RSI), the Parabolic System, and the Volatility Index (average true range or ATR) are true strokes of genius. The best of all, however, is the Directional Movement Index, known as the DMI, and its derivative, the Average Directional Movement Index (ADX). These two indicators have enormous power in the analysis of price trends. Their predictive abilities are amazing, yet I believe most traders use them in the wrong manner. After describing how they are calculated, I outline the most common mistakes that traders make in their interpretation of these two indicators and what I believe are the correct methods to use with them.

Wilder Moving Average and Average True Range (ATR)

Wilder used an unusual method of calculating a moving average. His book was written long before the availability of the personal computer, back in the days when all calculations were done by hand on preprinted spreadsheets. Because calculating by hand and using handheld adding machines were laborious, Wilder invented a new method of calculating a moving average that has some characteristics similar to what is today called an *exponential moving average*. He uses this moving average method in all his indicator calculations. If you use one of the indicators as calculated by one of the services available on the Internet, you must be sure that the vendor calculates the indicator with the same moving average method as Wilder. I'm not sure it makes much difference if a regular exponential moving average is used instead, but I like the idea of using the original method for purity and historical sake.

First, Wilder calculated what he called the *True Range* (TR). Price range is often calculated using the spread between the high and low each day. Thus, a stock with a high of 4 and a low of 3 would have a 1-point range. The average of these ranges over a specified period is then calculated and called the average trading range for the stock. However, Wilder believed that the normal method was insufficient because it did not include the price change between daily periods. He, thus, invented a new way of looking at price range and defined his daily true range as the greatest of the following:

- The price difference from today's high to today's low
- The price difference from yesterday's close to today's high
- The price difference from yesterday's close to today's low

His use of this method is now widely accepted as a measure of price volatility because it accounts for the trend in prices as well as the daily oscillation. Wilder was using daily data, but the true range can be calculated using any period data. Its uniqueness stems from its use of the previous bar's close. Rather than measure just the price action within one bar, it relates that one bar's price action to the previous bar. Often in trading markets, a bar will have prices completely out of the range of the previous bar, usually in the form of a gap. For example, if today's price traded between 3 and 4 and yesterday's high was 2 1/2, today's price would be outside the range of yesterday's price. This might not seem like an important point, but it is because it accounts for all the price change rather than just the price change within a specified period such as a day. A price change, as in the example, from 2 1/2 one day to 3 and 4 the next day is important but would not be picked up using only the price changes within each day.

Wilder calculated the average of the True Range using his special moving-average method. For a 14-day moving average, the period he used most often, the calculation is as follows:

Average True Range (ATR) is $ATR_{today} = ATR_{yesterday} - (ATR_{yesterday}/14) + TR_{today}$.

The starting point on the 14th day is a simple moving average of the TRs over the previous 14 days. The parameter of 14 can be changed to any number of days (bars).

These calculations introduce two important concepts:

1. Volatility covers two days (bars) rather than one and includes any gaps that might exist between days. It is, thus, more realistic as a volatility measure than standard deviation, beta, or most other volatility methods.

2. The moving average is not the sum of a number of days' figures divided by the number of days, but instead, is an average similar to an exponential that carries partial components of all previous days and adjusts the previous day's figure only by the current day's reading. Thus, there is no *drop-off effect* as exists, and is often a problem, in a simple moving average. The drop-off effect occurs in simple moving averages and any

oscillator that uses the figures at the beginning as well as the end of the period. It occurs when the old number is "dropped off" the average when the new number is added. If the number dropped off is a large number relative to others, it has a disproportionate effect on the average when it is subtracted from the average regardless of the size of the new number. By discounting old numbers rather than using them directly, the Wilder moving average reduces the drop-off effect.

Uses of the Average True Range

Entire trading systems have been developed around the ATR. The ATR represents the average bar volatility of the price. Figure 7.1 shows a daily bar chart with the average range percentage. The percentage is the ATR as a percent of its recent price and is the best calculation for comparing volatility between different stocks.

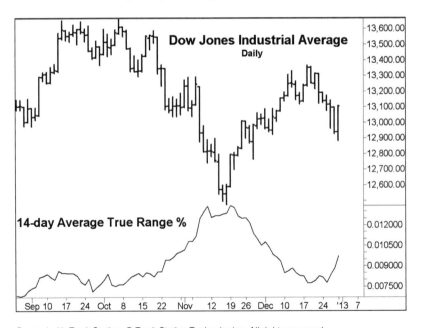

Figure 7.1   Fourteen-day Average True Range of the Dow Jones Industrial.

The ATR has multiple uses. Among them are the following:

- The ATR is often used as a means of estimating the future oscillations of the stock price. It is a measure of volatility. For example, if a stock is trending upward at a certain pace, its ATR will reflect the average oscillation about that trend. Should a daily price change occur outside that average oscillation, it may indicate a change in trend.

- The ATR is often used in the calculation of a trailing stop, an order that is placed to close a position if such an excessive outlier occurs. In a profitable long position, for example, a sell stop is placed a certain number of ATRs below the position's highest price while holding the stock. When that stop level is violated, it suggests that the trend upon which the profit has been generated is over, and the position should be closed.

- It is also used as an entry *breakout* signal for a stock price trading in a flat trend when it shows such aberrant behavior.

- A multiple of an ATR can be used as a *unit* to determine when margin should be used in pyramiding a trend-following system. For example, in the "Turtle System,"[2] a predetermined unit was a certain number of ATRs. Every time the price moved in the intended direction by a unit, an additional position was entered on margin. When the price moved adversely by a unit, the position was reduced.

- Because the ATR is a measure of volatility, its change, especially decline, is used in very short-term trading systems that depend on reduced volatility for their setup. A seven-bar, narrow-range (NR7) pattern, for example, is a common pattern for a directional trade. It develops when the ATR is lower than the ATR for the previous six bars. The trade occurs when the price breaks out from the high or low of the entire seven-bar pattern.

Directional Movement Index (DMI)

Wilder, like most traders, investigated how to analyze price trends. His studies focused on identifying when a trend was flat, and thus difficult to trade with trend-following systems, and when the trend was aggressive, and thus easy to profit from with trend-following systems. He believed that the price action within a bar and its relationship to the previous bar told him just how to do this. As a means of quantifying the relationship between price bars, he developed the Directional Movement Index (DMI; see Figure 7.2). It is a somewhat complicated series of calculations you will not need to perform yourself. Most Web-based chart services calculate and display various Wilder indicators on a price chart. You should understand the basic idea, however, of the relationship between price bars.

Wilder's Directional Movement
–DM and +DM

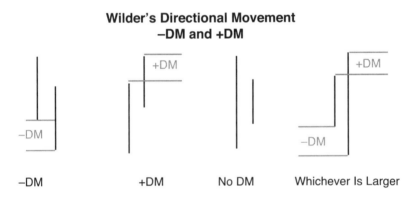

Source: Kirkpatrick, Charles, and Julie Dahlquist. *Technical Analysis*, 2nd ed. Upper Saddle River, NJ: FT Press, 2012.

Figure 7.2   Basis of Wilder's Directional Movement Index.

The Basic Element—The DM

To calculate the DM, the market action (any market) is observed over two days (bars). The DM, which stands for Directional Movement, can be either positive (+DM) or negative (–DM) depending on the relative position of the second day to the first. Its calculation is as follows:

- +DM occurs when the current high is higher than the high for the day before, an upward trend, and is measured as the difference in price between the two highs.

- −DM occurs when the current low is lower than the low for the day before, a downward trend, and is measured as *a positive number* and is the difference in price between the two lows.

- In situations where the current day's high is less than the high of the previous day and the low is greater than the low of the previous day, no recording is made for the DM, as the trend between the two days is neutral.

- In situations where the current day's high is greater than the previous day's high and the current day's low is lower than the previous day's low, called an *outside* day, the larger of the differences is used as the DM figure. When the high-to-high price difference is greater than the low-to-low price, the difference between the two differences is recorded as a +DM, a positive day. When the low-to-low figure is greater than the high-to-high figure, the difference between the two differences is recorded as a −DM, a negative day.

- Each day has only a +DM or a −DM recorded.

The Directional Index (DI)

Wilder used 14 days as the standard period, though any number of days or bars can be used. I will use 14 days for this demonstration:

1. First, over the past 14 days, sum the +DMs and the −DMs. This results in two columns, one representing the sum of all +DMs over the previous 14 days (called the $+DM_{14}$) and another column representing the sum of all −DMs (always a positive number) over the previous 14 days (called the $-DM_{14}$). These columns are updated with the Wilder Moving Average formula each day. Because each day must be either a +DM or −DM

day, when it is blank, just follow the formula without adding a new figure. The average will decline on its own.

2. To be realistic, the direction must be a function of the True Range to account for the price level and relative price motion within the specific security or average. Calculate the Average True Range over 14 days and divide each DM_{14} column by that range (called the TR_{14}). This produces the Directional Index (DI) for each column, the +DI and the –DI.

3. The +DI and –DI are the percentage of the average trading range over the past 14 days that was upward and downward. By comparing these figures, we know the directional force in the security. The total of upward and downward compared with the average range also tells us how much trending has occurred in the issue. A low percentage suggests that the issue's trend is flat. These figures (DI) can be plotted, and various trading rules have evolved about them.

Figure 7.3 shows examples of +DI and –DI: the +DI and –DI for the Dow Jones Industrial. Notice several things:

- Whichever DI is the larger of the two is telling us the direction of that trend. If the +DI is higher than the –DI, the trend is upward. In Figure 7.3, on December 31, 2012 (the last day), the –DI is above the +DI, indicating that the trend switched upward two days before (up arrow).

- A crossover in the two is thus a signal that the trend direction has changed from one to the other. Sometimes the +DI and –DI remain close to each other.

- The strength of the trend is the difference between +DI and –DI. In Figure 7.3, the recent downward trend is not as strong as the one, for example, in November when the –DI was considerably higher.

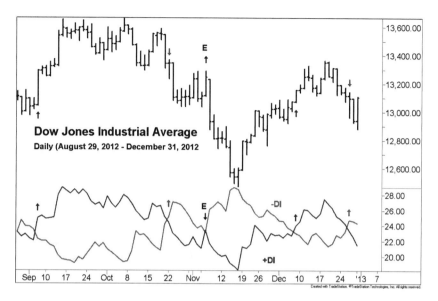

Figure 7.3   Dow Jones Industrial with +DI and –DI.

- A crossover is a setup for action. The rule for setup is that when a DI crosses its opposite DI, the price bar coincident with the crossover is the pattern breakout bar. A further break of that bar is the action signal when it occurs in the direction of the DI signal. In Figure 7.3, for example, all the crossovers are followed by price action in the direction of the crossover signal with the exception of the minor positive crossover at point "E." If the rule had been employed here, no action would have occurred because the price bar in the direction of the positive crossover was never broken. On the other hand, when the crossover became negative the next day, the crossover bar was broken downward and an action signal given to sell short.

- When the DI reaches a maximum extreme, it demonstrates that the trend is likely at its maximum slope and any position

associated with that trend should be watched closely. In Figure
7.3, the maximum for each DI appears to be around 28. When
that level was reached, it was the ideal time to close a trend
position because from then on, the odds suggest either a flat
trend or reversal.

- The DIs are used to calculate the ADX indicator, which I find
to be much more useful. As you can see from Figure 7.3, the
DI crossovers are late in their signals, and while the maximums
suggest closing a position, the DIs often don't reach their maximums, leaving you stranded.

Average Directional Movement Index (ADX)

Although I find the DIs useful, I like the Average Directional
Movement Index (ADX) for its insight into when a trend direction is
changing. It is uncanny in picking trend reversals, often within a few
bars of the peak or trough. The ADX is the primary indicator I use
in deciding when to act. It is a derivative calculation from the Directional Movement Index (DMI) mentioned previously and measures
the strength of a trend, not the direction. For this reason, it is sometimes difficult for traders to interpret because when the ADX is rising,
it signals that the strength of the trend is rising, not that the price is
rising. It acts like a second derivative that measures the acceleration
or deceleration of the trend rather than the slope of the trend. The
ADX is important for this reason because when it begins to change
direction, it signals that something important is happening to the
trend. When it peaks, for example, it usually indicates that the existing trend, up or down, is ending. Troughs indicate that the existing
trend is beginning to accelerate, up or down. It is, thus, an important
and indispensable indicator for the trend trader. Let me first outline
how it is calculated, but remember you will not have to perform these

calculations because the ADX is available in most Web-based chart services.

The Directional Index (DX)

The Wilder averages of DIs over 14 days are called the $+DI_{14}$ and $-DI_{14}$. The sum of $+DI_{14}$ and $-DI_{14}$ is the net percentage of the trend portion of the 14-day average trading range. If it is large, it tells us that the issue is trending strongly (up or down). Dividing the difference between $+DI_{14}$ and $-DI_{14}$ by the sum of $+DI_{14}$ and $-DI_{14}$ gives us the percentage of trending in the issue in one direction or the other called the *DX*. It doesn't tell us the direction, only the strength of that portion of the Average True Range that is trending. To make it a true percentage, multiply the answer by 100.

For example, an upward trending stock with a $+DI_{14}$ of 45 and a $-DI_{14}$ of 13 would have a plurality of 32% of the trading range that is trending. Dividing 32 by the sum of trending (45+13) or 58 gives us the DX on that day for that stock. The percentage of directional trending is, therefore, 32/58 or 0.552 (55.2%). This is a strongly trending stock because over 55% of the trading range is accounted for by trending.

The Average Directional Movement Index (ADX)

The Average Directional Movement Index uses a different Wilder Average formula over 14 days. That equation is as follows:

$$ADX_{today} = (ADX_{previous} \times 13 + DX_{today}) / 14$$

The Average Directional Movement Rating (ADXR) is calculated as the difference between the current ADX and the ADX 14 days prior. It dampens the natural, shorter-term oscillations in trend strength displayed by the ADX. Figure 7.4 shows the ADX with the ADXR.

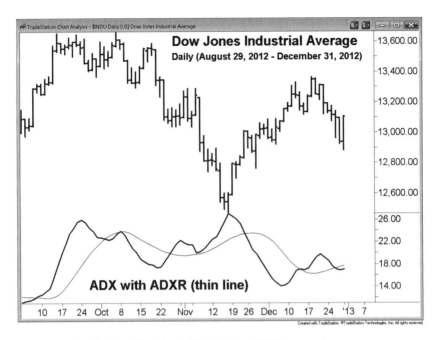

Figure 7.4 Dow Jones Industrial with ADX and ADXR.

Wilder's Rules for the DIs and ADX

In Wilder's book, he outlines his analysis and use of the Directional Movement Index and its components. They are interesting from a historical perspective, but I have tested them all and found them difficult to profit from. These rules are the following:

- When the ADXR is above 25, the crossover in the DI is a signal in the direction of the crossover. Use the extreme point on the price for the day of crossing as an entry stop level.

- When the ADX rises above the highest DI, a turning point is indicated. The turning point often occurs concurrent with the first downturn in the ADX after the ADX has crossed above both DI lines.

- When the ADX declines below both DI lines, it is time to stop trading a trend-following system. No trend exists worth trading with a low ADX.

- Sort issues on their ADXR. The highest ratings are the strongest trending issues.

How to Use the ADX

You will notice that Wilder was concerned about the level of the ADX rather than its turning points. He knows that a peak is important, especially when it is a high level (above the DI). This preoccupation with numerical level of the ADX is common in other articles and writings about the ADX, but I have found it to be mostly irrelevant. The important aspect of the ADX is its ability to peak at the end of a trend and thus provide a signal to close a position regardless of its numerical value. In Figure 7.5, I show a chart of the Dow Jones Industrial and its ADX with the ADX peaks marked and their corresponding price extremes. In every ADX peak, the price chart shows either a top or a bottom regardless of the ADX value. In only one instance, the first bottom signal, does the price fail soon after the ADX peak indicates a price trend reversal.

As an indicator of when to close a trend-following position, the ADX is superb. As an indicator of entry in a new trend, the ADX peak must be used with caution. The only caveat in determining an ADX peak is that often the ADX will make minor wrinkles that at first might mistakenly be interpreted as a peak. To reduce this risk of a false interpretation, I use a reversal amount to confirm that a peak has occurred. This takes a few more bars of price action and thus the possibility of being late in closing a position, but I am more confident that the closing is reliable.

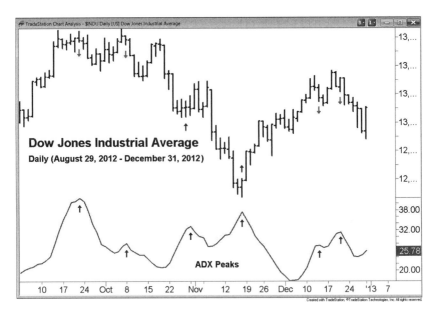

Figure 7.5   Dow Jones Industrial with ADX peaks.

As an example, in Figure 7.5, I suggest you look at the second-to-last, small ADX peak in December. In general and by definition, an ADX peak is not recognized until at least the close of the bar after the peak, call it "bar 2." Usually, it is the second bar that determines the peak by suddenly moving in the direction opposite to the trend. That a real ADX peak has occurred can be confirmed two ways: (1) The ADX declines by a certain, pretested amount, or (2) the price breaks the bar 2 high or low depending on the new direction signaled. In the example, the ADX peak occurred with a down bar (at the down arrow). It was not known to be a peak, however, until the next bar (bar 2), which was also a down bar. The ADX did not decline by any large amount—and is therefore suspicious—and the bar 2 low was never penetrated. Thus, the second-from-the-last ADX in the chart would not have been legitimate and should not have been acted upon. The same analysis would not have saved a failed long trade at the ADX peak in late October. Here, the ADX retraced a large amount and would likely have passed that test. Bar 2, however, did not rally very strongly, which might have been a clue that the pattern would fail, but the following bar 3 certainly confirmed the ADX peak and price bottom. It failed, however. The lesson is that in this type of ADX system, a protective stop is necessary in case of failure. The other aspect of such a system, as is true of all ADX systems, is that the exit strategy cannot wait for an opposite directional ADX signal. The system is not a "stop-and-reverse" system. The exit must be either on a trailing stop or a price or time target. In most of my tests, I use a time target.

Another method of confirming an ADX peak is the use of the ADXR as a signal line, similar to how a signal line is used in the Moving Average Convergence Divergence (MACD) indicator. In the ADX, the signal of an ADX peak is when the ADX crosses below the ADXR. In Figure 7.4, the ADX crosses below the ADXR four times. The first and second crossover (the second is very small) mark the market price peak very well. The third downward crossover signals the market bottom nicely, though somewhat late. The final crossover will turn out to be disastrous, thus requiring the protective stop in any strategy using this system. My criticism of using the ADXR is that it is late and not more accurate than the raw ADX peak. In addition and similar to the whipsaws that can occur in a moving-average crossover system, when the ADX itself becomes flat, it crosses back and forth over the ADXR frequently and thus gives multiple false signals. For these reasons, I don't use the ADXR as a signal line. Wilder also mentions using the ADXR as a sort for the strongest trending stocks. I have not tested that because relative price strength as calculated in Chapter 2, "Investment Strategies: Backtesting," provides a more precise and tested screen.

The most intriguing and almost-never-used aspect of the ADX is when it reaches a bottom and reverses upward. Most commentators, including Wilder, never mention the usefulness of an ADX trough. The prevailing opinion that a strong ADX is desirable and a weak, downward trend in the ADX is something to avoid has missed an important and profitable indicator. A trough in the ADX occurs after a trend has weakened in strength but not necessarily in direction. In Figure 7.5, for example, the entire advance in the Dow Jones Industrial from the price bottom in mid-November was accompanied by a declining ADX. Thus, the declining ADX was not a cause for worry. Notice, however, that when the ADX formed a trough in early December, the price rise in the market accelerated. This is the nature of the ADX as a signal. The rising ADX is a sign of acceleration in the direction of the trend but not a sign that the trend should be exited. That only occurs when the rising ADX forms a peak. When the ADX forms a trough, it suggests that the existing trend is accelerating and is, thus, the signal that a second trade in the direction of the trend could be profitable. In Figure 7.6, I marked all the ADX lows with corresponding arrows on the price chart. The first ADX trough was a failure because the price soon after broke down. The second ADX trough was a sign that the decline was accelerating and was a good time to sell short. The third ADX trough in early November repeated the second bearish signal and was also a profitable entry point. The fourth ADX trough occurred after an ADX peak and coincident market bottom and was also an excellent entry signal. Thus, while the ADX trough is not a reversal signal, it still is a profitable method of taking advantage of a trend.

The one caveat in using the ADX trough for signals is that it must emphasize the existing trend. If the existing trend is upward, the signal reinforces it, but you must be sure of the trend direction. In Figure 7.6, I use the forward line (to be discussed in more detail in Chapter 8, "Cycles and the Forward Line") as a means of standardizing identification of the trend. The DMI could be used in a similar manner.

If the price is above the forward line, I know the trend is upward and that any ADX trough will signal a time to buy. Conversely, when the price is below the forward line, I know the trend is downward and that any ADX trough will signal a time to sell short.

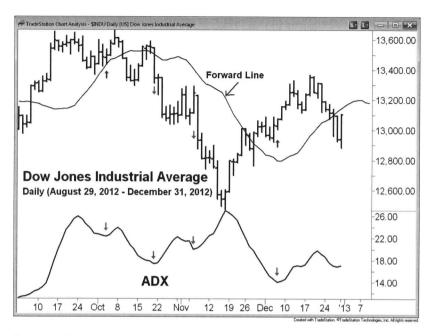

Figure 7.6   Dow Jones Industrial with ADX troughs.

As in determining an ADX peak, the determination of an ADX trough must consider the amount by which the ADX has reversed as well as confirmation in the trend direction by the price breaking bar 2 in that direction. In addition, the use of an ADX trough as an entry signal must utilize another means of closing the position either through stops or targets. It is not a "stop-and-reverse" system.

Conclusion

Wilder's invention of the DMI and the ADX is one of the great technical achievements of all time. It is simple to calculate, and it encompasses the reasonable assumption that bar-to-bar change reflects underlying price strength or weakness. This internal strength or weakness determines the trend and by manipulation the strength of that trend. From these deductions, the ADX, especially, is a prime indicator of trend direction, trend acceleration, and trend reversal—the exact requirements of a trend trader or investor. In real life, it has proven to be a profitable indicator when applied correctly and with caution. It is my favorite.

Endnotes

1. Wilder, J. Welles Jr. *New Concepts in Technical Trading Systems.* Greensboro, NC: Trend Research, 1978.

2. Faith, Curtis. *Way of the Turtle: The Secret Methods That Turned Ordinary People into Legendary Traders.* New York, NY: McGraw-Hill, 2007.

8

Cycles and the Forward Line

When I was first involved in technical analysis in the 1960s, looking for patterns in the price charts was the basic means of analyzing stocks or any freely traded security. I learned point-and-figure first from books from Abe Cohen[1] and from Earl Blumenthal[2] on three-point reversal charts, and about one-point reversals from Alexander Wheelan.[3] I learned about bar charts from William Jiler in his 1962 book, *How Charts Can Help You in the Stock Market*[4] and from Edwards and Magee.[5] Because there were only hand-operated adding machines for calculators in those days, and no spreadsheets, I cranked through rolls of paper with moving-average calculations of breadth figures and index prices, but never seemed to get anywhere helpful. I truly hated moving averages for the work they created and the limited and always-late signals they gave when they crossed or turned.

It wasn't until 1970 when Jim Hurst wrote his famous book on cycles called the *Profit Magic of Stock Market Timing*[6] that I considered the use of moving averages with any seriousness. At that time, I was a member of the *Foundation for the Study of Cycles*, which had been formed in 1941 by Edward R. Dewey, an early chief economist to President Hoover. At various times during its existence, some famous economists like Wesley Mitchell of the Federal Reserve, Ellsworth Huntington of Yale, and Professor G. C. Abbott of the University of Virginia were members. Even Edward Johnson, the founder of Fidelity Investments, was on the Board of Directors at one point. In fact, as I became more interested in and studied the possibility that markets have some harmonic components, I spoke several times at their seminars on the Kondratieff 50+-year cycle and the 4-year cycle in stock prices. But Hurst's book was an eye-opener because it showed for the first time how to analyze prices for cycles and, even more exciting, how to make money using them. Hurst taught an educational course on his method, and I attended one in Washington DC to learn firsthand how his method worked. Recently, Christopher Grafton has written an excellent book, *Mastering Hurst Cycle Analysis*,[7] that explains Hurst's methods in modern, computer-adaptable detail.

Why be interested in cycles? Aside from the obvious purpose of finding a way to make money, if cycles existed in price data, I could predict as well as react by using them. Technical analysis doesn't predict; classically, it establishes the entry point in a trade or investment as a trigger to a previously recognized setup, and the closing of a trade is rarely done as the result of a target or predetermined time being reached. Both entry and exit are performed as a reaction to how prices behave. It's a mistake to suggest that technical analysts "forecast." They don't. They only gauge whether a particular security is attractive and wait for it to "break out" of a pattern or support or resistance level. Cycles, on the other hand, offer the possibility of actually predicting future price action. Cycles are strictly mathematical, whereas most technical and fundamental indicators are not. It seemed to me to possibly beat the system with some precision.

Cyclicality in Prices

Both Hurst and Dewey theorized that the market is a composite of various-length cycles. They believed that trading market prices were especially susceptible to cyclical effects but were unable to arrive at a reason. A reason for the existence of cycles isn't absolutely necessary to believe in what is observed empirically, though it is certainly more comforting to know "why" cycles exist. If their existence can be demonstrated empirically, the "why" can come later. The sun rose and set every day without explanation for millions of years, but only in the past 1,000 or so years has its transit been understood. Despite his lack of solar knowledge, the caveman could still accurately predict with reliability that the sun would rise the next morning. Thus, in trading markets, if cycles exist, we don't know why, but still we can use what we have observed to analyze and predict.

The most commonly observed cycle in stock prices is the so-called "Presidential" cycle of roughly four years from trough to trough. We also know that an annual cycle exists, especially in agricultural products, as would be expected from the annual growing cycle.

Both Hurst and Dewey wrote about how cycles tend to harmonize, that is occur in lengths that are whole-number multiples of shorter cycles. This means that a cycle will consist of shorter cycles of a length easily divisible by 2 or 3 or some other whole number. For example, a cycle of 18 months duration seems to exist within each four-year cycle, and it is one-third of four years. Each 18-month cycle, in turn, is composed of two 9-month cycles, and each of them is composed of three 3-months cycles, known otherwise as quarterly cycles for earnings reporting. This harmonic progression continues downward to just minutes of trading activity. The multiplier need not be 2 or 3, but the multiplier is always a whole number.

In market price data, I believe cycles are only tendencies, not facts. If cycles exist in market data, they are not very precise. Were they precise, they would have been quantified many years ago. However, there does seem to be a tendency toward periodicity in stock prices. That means the market highs and lows have a habit of occurring at regular intervals regardless of their strength and underlying trend.

Cycles

Cycles can be defined mathematically using trigonometric functions, specifically the sine and cosine formulas. For this reason, the mathematics of discovery are well understood, and cycles can be pulled out of time series data with ease using Fourier transforms, spectral analysis, or digital filtering. Why don't these methods work in the stock market? Because although stock prices have a periodicity to their price action, the amplitude of their oscillations is not constant, and most mathematics-based trigonometric functions assume constant amplitude. Figure 8.1 displays an ideal cycle as defined by a sine curve.

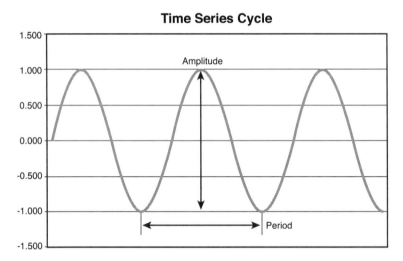

Figure 8.1   Idealized cycle appearance.

A cycle is defined by four variables: the period, the amplitude, the phase shift, and the vertical shift. The shifts refer to the cycle's starting point; the amplitude is the height of the cycle from bottom to top; and the period is the distance in time from one low to the next. In the stock market, the period between cycles is of most interest to traders, and the amplitude, the projected peak or trough level, is of interest only to a limited extent because it is based on volatility and is, thus, irregular.

When a cycle is duplicated to the right by half a cycle period, it behaves identically to the cycle only a half cycle distance to the right. This new cycle is called a *forward line.* When carried back and overlaid over the actual cycle, the half cycle move forward makes the forward line appear as a mirror image of the actual cycle, but in cycle time, its direction and value are almost always opposite from the actual cycle. In Figure 8.2, you can see that the peaks and troughs in the forward line (dashed line) appear exactly at the same levels as the actual cycle peaks and troughs (solid line) but halfway through the cycle. You can also see that when the cycle moves through a forward line, it does so at the halfway point of the distance from top to bottom or bottom to top. This implies that when a price breaks through its forward line, it will travel a distance equal to the distance it traveled to reach the break point. The breakthrough, thus, establishes a price target for the next cycle.

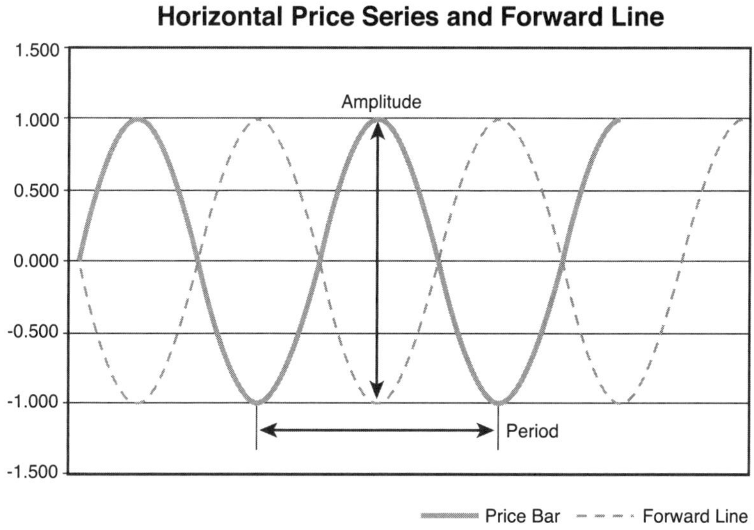

Horizontal Price Series and Forward Line

Figure 8.2 Centered moving average and forward line.

Of course, such analysis assumes a flat market without the effect of a large cycle or trend influencing the relative locations of the amplitude and crossovers. Figure 8.3 shows how the forward line acts during a strong advance.

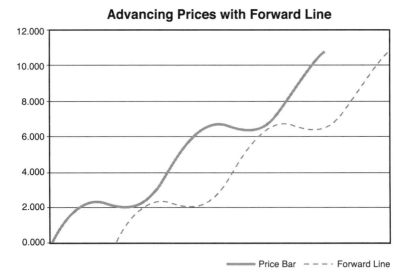

Figure 8.3 Forward line in a strong advance.

Notice in Figure 8.3 that if the trend is strongly upward, the price never crosses the forward line and, thus, a target is not possible to calculate. We can use this characteristic in real prices not only to show that a trend is very strong, but also to use the forward line as a sell stop level because breaking it indicates that the trend is no longer strong.

All analysis of cycles includes analysis of the next longer cycle or the underlying trend. It is the direction and strength of that trend that I want to know in order to profit from cycle analysis. I am interested in the specific cycle only in so far as it tells me what its underlying trend is doing and whether that underlying trend's strength is shifting. I do this by looking at the following:

- **The last cycle low level compared with the previous cycle low in an upward trend**—A succession of higher lows indicates the trend is upward, and the breaking of a prior cycle trough indicates that the trend is reversing downward. In a downward trend, the succession of lower cycle peaks indicates a downward trend. A period of irregular peaks and troughs indicates a flat trend and the likelihood that a technical pattern is forming.

- **The translation of the cycle**—Translation refers to where the peak in the cycle occurs between each low. All stock market cycle periods are measured from low to low. The peaks can occur at irregular intervals based on the underlying trend. If the trend is upward, the peak is to the right of the center of the cycle. You can see in Figure 8.3 how each cycle peak is slightly to the right of the cycle center. This skew is called *translation* and is useful in determining if the underlying trend is still healthy. If the peak is beyond the halfway point in the cycle, the translation is to the right, and the trend is still upward. If the peak within a cycle occurs early in the cycle, it suggests that the underlying trend is downward. How would you know the peak was early? Only by seeing the price break below the previous cycle trough in the first half of the current cycle. At that point, it is unquestionable that the underlying trend has turned downward. By watching translation, I can thus reinforce my understanding of the trend direction and any changes in it. The opposite interpretation is valid during a downward trend where the sequence of cycle peaks is lower. An upward break of the most recent peak indicates that the longer-term trend is now upward.

- **The possibility of an inversion**—In the stock market, cycle periods are fairly steady and troughs occur on schedule, but troughs don't always occur at the expected periodic interval. Sometimes peaks occur when a trough is expected. This is called an *inversion* and is relatively rare. It occurs when a longer-term underlying trend is rising but about to reverse direction. It is often accompanied by an ADX peak. An inversion is a frustrating event because it brings into doubt my analysis of the cyclical periods. I've found that continuing with the original interpretation of cycle period and assuming that the sequence of troughs will return to the earlier schedule is the best solution. It is unusual for an inversion to upset the rhythm of the cycles. Inversions cannot occur at troughs.

- **A price target**—In an upward trend, if the price target is established and the next peak fails to reach that target, I have the indication that the upward trend is slowing in momentum. If the target is exceeded by a large margin, I know that the underlying trend is accelerating. This is usually accompanied by an upturn in the ADX. In a downward trend, the relationship of the target price and the trough has the same implications as in an upward trend. Failure to reach a downside target suggests the trend is turning upward and exceeding the target is a sign of downward acceleration. As in the upward trend, if the target is exceeded, the ADX will likely turn upward.

Plotting and Understanding Moving Averages

Most of the methods described in this book require a length for an indicator. The Directional Movement Index (DMI), Average Directional Movement Index (ADX), and Average True Movement Indicator Range (ATR) all require a length over which the indicator travels. Different lengths in indicators have different results. It is important that the length of an indicator is related to the price action of the stock. Most indicators have their standard lengths, but in many cases these standards were not developed by any investigative approach. Most of the standards were developed before the advent of the computer and because they were easy to calculate on an adding machine. I've found instead that indicator lengths should be directly related to the cycle period of the prices being investigated. It is, therefore, imperative that I have a means of quantifying a cycle period. Underlying all my studies is recognizing what cycles are occurring in the market, and to profit from them, I need to understand how to calculate cycle periods.

Cycle Period Calculations

There are two methods of determining cycle length. The first is the use of moving averages, and the second is by trial and error.

As I mentioned in Chapter 4, "Market Timing and Walk-Forward Optimizing," in discussing crossover systems, moving averages dampen the minor fluctuations in price series data and allow the longer trends or cycles to appear more clearly. They are the primary means of observing and calculating cycle periods.

An average is the sum of numbers divided by the amount of numbers in the sum. Thus, a 25-day average of closing prices is the sum of closing prices over 25 days divided by 25. It is also called the *mean*. A moving average is that same average calculated each new day and drawn on a price graph along with the price. Figure 8.4 shows a daily plot for the Exchange Traded Fund (ETF) of the Standard & Poor's 500 Index (symbol = SPY) over a period just short of a year.

If we think of the market as a composite of various-length cycles, we can use the characteristics of moving averages to our advantage. Because moving averages reduce the effect of fluctuations shorter than their length, a 25-day moving average reduces the short-term fluctuations or cycles of 25 days and less and emphasizes the longer cycles in the price data. I chose the 25-day moving average for a reason. There is a 25–26 day cycle in the SPY. The moving average in its capacity to dampen out fluctuations of less than its length reduces the 25-day cycle fluctuations to a line on the chart with a much longer cycle identified by the low May and November. This longer cycle period is approximately 122 days, a multiple of the 25-day cycle by five. But we are interested in the shorter cycle in this discourse and can disregard the longer cycle for now.

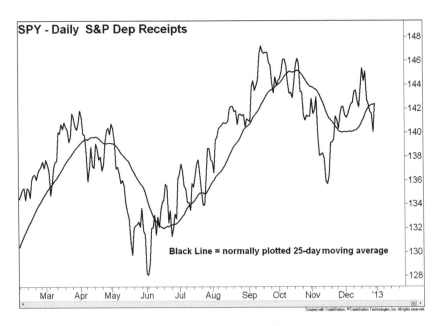

SPY - Daily S&P Dep Receipts

Black Line = normally plotted 25-day moving average

Figure 8.4   Normal rendition of a price chart with a moving average. Twenty-five-day moving average of the Standard & Poor's 500 Exchange Traded Fund [SPY] from February 2012 to December 2012.

Plotting a moving average coincident with the most recent price, however, is not strictly accurate because the average price actually occurs not on the most recent day but on the average day sometime in the past. More realistically, a moving average should be plotted at the mean day as well as the mean price. In the 25-day moving average, think of the 25 days as a box that is 25 days wide and so many points high to represent the price range. The moving average should be the average of both the height (the price) and the width (the time). The plot should be in the middle of the box 12.5 days earlier than the present and at the price average. I can't plot at 12.5 days past and must round the number of days to 13. This adjusted plot is called a *centered moving average* to distinguish it from the more common moving average normally seen in price charts.

Figure 8.5 is a daily plot of the SPY with its 25-day centered moving average plotted correctly. Notice that because the average is a centered moving average in time as well as price, the average itself tracks almost exactly the price curve. It turns when the price curve turns, peaks when it peaks, and troughs when it troughs. The major problem there is that it is 13 days late, and because a 25-day moving average is late to turn anyway because it takes roughly 12 days of numbers to change its direction, the value of the centered moving average is limited as an indicator alone for trading market turns. But Hurst found some interesting aspects of the centered moving average that I will discuss as I move along toward the construction and use of the forward line.

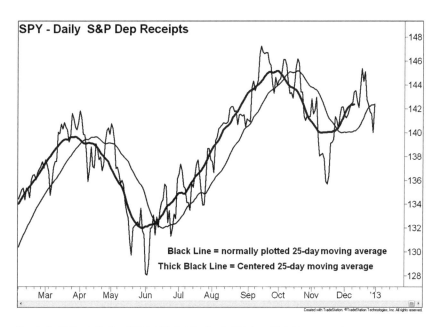

Figure 8.5 Twenty-five-day centered moving average.

Figure 8.6 shows SPY over the same period as shown in Figures 8.4 and 8.5 and displays its center line and its forward line. This is a chart similar to the ideal cycle plotted in Figure 8.3 only with real prices and a slightly upward slope. Notice that the forward line parallels the centered moving average, which represents the actual cycle in SPY, and peaks and troughs at the same level as the cycle peaks and troughs in the real cycle. Notice also that the forward line extends into the future ahead of the last reported price. We now have a moving average that actually leads prices and tells us something about the future rather than just about the past. Finally, notice that the forward line acts as a stopping point, a support or resistance level, to prices. In December, the price bounced directly off the forward line; in early October, it also bounced off the forward line, and all the corrections in the period from June to September were contained above the forward line.

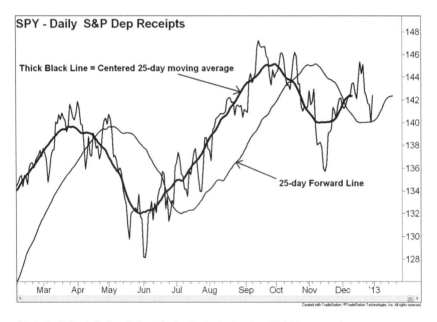

Figure 8.6   Twenty-five-day centered moving average and 25-day forward line placed 13 days ahead.

Buy and sell crossover signals occurred when price broke through the forward line. The first of these signals occurred in April when the price broke below the forward line. This break didn't indicate that the trend was reversing, only that the upward trend had ended. Eventually, the price broke the earlier low and the trend turned downward. In June, during the decline, the price attempted to break above the forward line but failed. In its attempt to break the forward line, it did break above a previous high, thus suggesting that the downward trend had ended. Finally, it broke upward through the forward line and remained above it until it broke its rising forward line and a previous price trough in October. At this point, traders should have sold. The subsequent rally up through the forward line failed to reach new highs, suggesting that the trend was now flat, and in late October, the price again broke below a previous low as well as its forward line, indicating a new downward trend. In December, the price broke up through its forward line and several days later broke above a prior peak, thus establishing an upward trend. Notice that on the last day of the year, just before an enormous upward trend, the correction failed to break below the forward line. In this respect, the forward line acted as a brake to the decline.

As for the usefulness of projections using the forward line as a halfway point, notice that the earlier high in March had suggested a large decline was likely based on the distance from the forward line projected lower. This decline did not occur and the correction below the forward line was small but projected only a small advance above the forward line for the next rally. The rally fell far short of its price objective, suggesting that the correction earlier indicated was about to occur.

As for the particulars of trading with the forward line, you will notice that the price often breaks the line for only a day and then reverses. The trading method of handling this false breakout is to place a "fudge" factor or filter at the crossover day's high or low on the following day depending on the direction of the forward line break. If that price plus the fudge factor is broken, the breakout is likely valid and the trend has changed. Such a method would have kept you from selling prematurely in April until the final break in early May at a higher price. It would have kept you from buying on the upward breakout of the forward line in June and given you a better price later in June, and, depending on the amount of the fudge factor, might have prevented a premature sale in October on the first downward crossover.

I think it is obvious that the forward line has value in confirming trend direction, though I admit it is difficult to profit from forward lines alone. As a background trend check, however, it is superb. Generally, when the price is above the forward line, the trend is upward, and vice versa when the price is below the forward line. Because the signals occur late, they are not particularly useful by themselves except as confirmation of other signals. When I combine the forward line with the DMI and ADX, however, I get a much clearer and immediate picture with actual action signals. For example, an ADX low, which very few analysts use as a signal, is excellent in pinpointing a continued directional move based on whether prices are above or below their forward line. If above, and the ADX turns upward, the price will likely accelerate upward, and conversely, when the price is below the forward line, an ADX upturn is an excellent short sale.

A moving average dampens out any cycle lesser than its length, and the raw daily data includes all cycles. Thus, if we subtract the moving average from the raw data, we get a horizontal line with daily oscillations about it. This is shown in Figure 8.7 as a ratio of the daily data to the 25-day centered moving average. The moving average plot must be centered; otherwise, the ratio will not represent the actual figures for specific days and will skew the results. This chart now displays all the cycles at or shorter than 25 days. I have drawn vertical lines at obvious low points in the chart to show the periodicity of lows in the SPY prices. The distance between each low is 25 days with a few days error at some troughs. This exercise then proves that the SPY has a tendency to bottom every 25 days. With that knowledge, we can construct a forward line as well as use the 25-day period for the period calculations in all our other technical indicators such as the DMI and ADX. This is the great value in interpreting cycles.

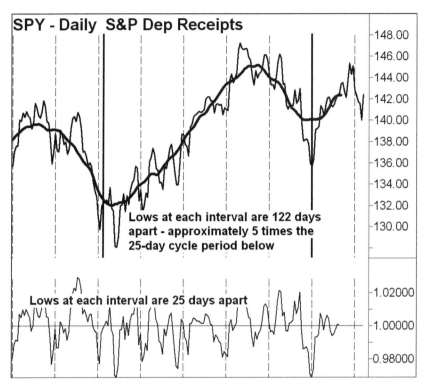

SPY - Daily S&P Dep Receipts

Lows at each interval are 122 days apart - approximately 5 times the 25-day cycle period below

Lows at each interval are 25 days apart

Figure 8.7   Ratio of current price to the centered moving average.

The other method of trial and error uses a moving average and forward line placed half the length of the moving average forward of the current price. By adjusting the moving average length until the forward line just traces the highs and lows of actual prices in the past, I get the correct length to use in the moving average and other indicators. For example, using the same chart of SPY, by adjusting the length of the moving average from 25 to 29, the picture in Figure 8.8 changes considerably and many of the false signals no longer occur. This moving average now projects the forward line 15 days ahead. To simplify calculations, I always use an odd number for the moving average because the midpoint is always a whole number. Thus, with a 25-day average, the midpoint is day 13, and with a 29-day moving average, the midpoint is day 15. The formula for the forward line advance is 1/2 the moving average plus 0.5.

Figure 8.8   Twenty-nine-day moving average moved ahead 15 days.

Conclusion

When trading price trends, it is important to be able to quantify several necessary items. The first is to quantify the trend itself. The forward line provides a reliable way to do that. Second, all technical indicators require a length calculation in their makeup. The length can be arbitrary or more logically the length can be relative to the trading cycle of interest. Cycle analysis provides this information. Finally, although there are more sophisticated methods to be used with cycles, the Hurst[8] method and the Tillman[9] method being the best, I prefer to use cycles only in the general sense because of my skepticism about the precision needed but lacking in cycle analysis.

Endnotes

1. Cohen, Abe. *The Chartcraft Method of Point and Figure Trading*. Larchmont, NY: Chartcraft, 1960.

2. Blumenthal, Earl. *Chart for Profit Point and Figure Trading*. Larchmont, NY: Investors Intelligence, 1975.

3. Wheelan, Alexander H. *Study Helps in Point and Figure Technique*. New York, NY: Morgan, Rogers and Roberts, 1954.

4. Jiler, William. *How Charts Can Help You in the Stock Market*. New York, NY: Commodity Research Corporation, 1962.

5. Edwards, Robert, and John Magee. *Technical Analysis of Stock Trends*. 9th ed. Boca Raton, FL: CRC Press, 2007. (Original edition, 1948)

6. Hurst, James M. *The Profit Magic of Stock Transaction Timing*. Englewood Cliffs, NJ: Prentice-Hall, 1970.

7. Grafton, Christopher. *Mastering Hurst Cycle Analysis*. Petersfield, Hampshire, Great Britain: Harriman House, 2011.

8. Ibid.

9. Kirkpatrick, Charles, and Julie Dahlquist. *Technical Analysis: The Complete Resource for Financial Market Technicians*. 2nd ed. Upper Saddle River, NJ: FT Press, 2011, pages 472–74.

9

Trading Models and Tests

The trading indicators and methods described in Chapters 7 and 8, "Directional Movement Index (DMI) and the ADX" and "Cycles and the Forward Line," respectively, are now combined into trading models. I prefer to use my own interpretation of a chart with all the indicators displayed but to learn the nuances in the beginning, the best method for the student is to use a checklist of what indicators to look for. Deciding on action should be based on the configuration of the indicators, specifically the direction of the trend and the more subtle indications of timing entries and exits.

I follow about 20 stocks closely. I selected them for their volatility and liquidity. Liquidity is usually measured by dollar trading volume and volatility by the percentage Average True Range (ATR)—for ATR calculation, see Chapter 7. I like to see at least $10 million per day on average, over the past 50 days, and an ATR on top of all stocks with that volume of transactions. I almost never know what the company behind the stock does for business. I don't wish to be wedded to an idea. I also don't care about the trend of the stock. The trend direction can be traded either way. The only problem with a stock that has trended downward for any length of time is that stock may not be available for borrowing because it has already been sold short. I check with my brokerage firm before following any stock in such a position because with no stock available, I cannot sell it short. I don't like stocks with huge price gaps because it suggests a large institutional following that can turn fickle overnight. I don't really care about price either except that it is difficult to sell short stocks under $5 per share.

Requirement for Period in All Indicators

Stochastic, Relative Strength Index (RSI), Moving Average Convergence Divergence (MACD), and most other technical indicators require a period length for their calculation. It only makes sense that the periods for an indicator reflect the period of its trading cycle. This is the reason for the exercise in determining the cycle period. Most indicators relate directly to the trading cycle of the underlying security. If the security has a 23-day cycle, the indicator length should be 23 days or half the cycle at 13 days. Often half-cycle periods are better because they are more sensitive than the longer period. In the forward line projection, the forward line is the moving average, full- or half-cycle period, advanced a half-cycle period ahead of current prices. The projection is a half cycle regardless of how the representative moving average is calculated. It is the cycle period that determines the displacement of the forward line, not the period of the moving average.

Determining Cycle Length

Hurst outlined the nominal, as opposed to the real, cycle lengths in stock market data. In daily data, they are 10, 20, 40, and 80 days. These are the starting points in the search for the real cycle period. The search method is to calculate a 10-day centered moving average followed by a ratio of the current price to that moving average. By looking at the results, you will see if there is a cycle in the data. It will appear as a series of sharp lows at equidistant periods. If the plot doesn't show any clear series of sequential, equally spaced lows, there probably isn't a cycle with a length around 10. Do the same calculations using a 20-day moving average and see if any cycle pops out to your eyes. If it does, the actual period between lows is the cycle length and the figure to be used for further calculations. If it is not obvious where the cyclical lows occur, then continue up the ladder of nominal lengths until you find a cycle. That cycle length or a half of the cycle length is your new period length for your indicators. If you don't find any cycle in the price data, you should probably disregard the security because its behavior is too erratic. Figure 9.1, for example, is a chart showing the method of using the ratio of the close to a 10-bar centered moving average, one of Hurst's nominal cycles, to determine the 26-hour cycle in the chart of the SPY.

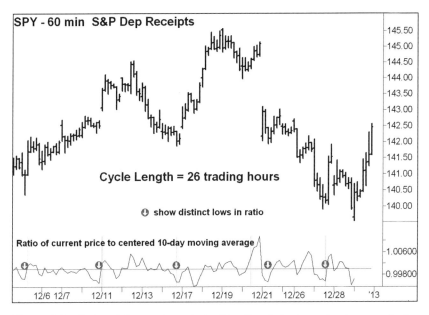

Figure 9.1   Determining cycle period with ratio of closing price to a nominal period (10 trading hours) centered moving average and showing a 26-hour cycle in the price data (S&P ETF [SPY] December 4–31, 2012).

Once you have found the cycle length, you now have the period lengths to use in any of your indicators. I generally use a half-cycle period on moving averages, the forward line, the Directional Movement Index (DMI), and the Average Directional Movement Index (ADX), but if you prefer additional indicators, you now have a method to determine the length to substitute in their formulas.

Three-Bar Reversal

One indicator I omitted earlier but is important to the trading system is the three-bar reversal (see examples in Figure 9.2). In classical technical analysis theory, the concept of support and resistance is important. These are price zones where a security's price has stopped in its trend and reversed direction. In theory, the reversal in direction is due to the change in balance between buyers and sellers. During a price advance, for example, buyers are in control and are more aggressive than sellers, thus the price rises. When the price stops rising and reverses downward, the implication from the price trend reversal is that sellers have now taken control and are more aggressive. Something happened at that price where the reversal occurred. In the future, that price level often becomes a barrier to future advances because there have been and presumably will be an excess of sellers at that level. The name for this is the *resistance* level, and its opposite where a price decline halts and reverses upward is referred to as the *support* level. It would seem a simple exercise to identify each support and resistance, but in some cases, the levels are not clear and thus require an easily applied formula. I use the *three-bar reversal* to identify one or the other level.

In a price chart with a declining trend, for example, any bar with a low price below the three bars preceding that bar and the three bars following has a three-bar reversal low. The *three* refers to the number of adjacent bars on either side of the low bar that have price lows above the center bar low. A bar reversal is not limited to three bars. You could have a five-bar reversal or a one-bar reversal, for example. The number of required bars determines the importance and frequency of the pattern. A large number of bars occur less frequently, but is more important than a reversal bar with few bars. Likewise, a reversal bar with only a few adjacent bars occurs frequently and is of less importance. I use three bars because I find it to be the best compromise. A three-bar reversal low is significant enough to have withstood the pressure of sellers for at least seven bars and thus is an important low. It is a support level. We know that in the past buyers entered the market at that price, absorbed the sellers, and overwhelmed them enough to reverse the price trend upward. In the future, we expect them to enter again at that price.

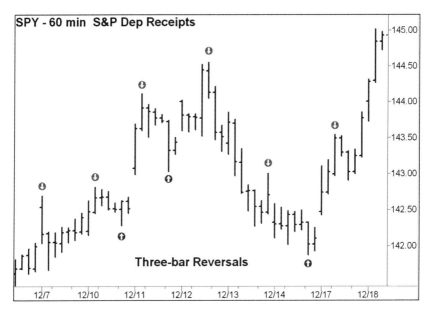

Figure 9.2   Three-bar reversals—note that each peak is surrounded on each side by three adjacent bars with lower highs, and that each three-bar low is surrounded on each side by three adjacent bars with higher lows. Bars with only two adjacent bars higher or lower do not qualify (S&P 500 ETF [SPY], December 6–18, 2012).

If during a subsequent price decline the buyers do not enter at that price, however, the price will break below that three-bar reversal low price, and we can expect the price to continue lower until it reaches another support level at a lower price. The price is said to have "broken down" out of the support level. Because the breakout indicates a change in supply and demand for the stock, it is an important signal, one that I prefer to see accompanying other signals in the same direction as the breakout.

Analysis Sequence

The chart I use has the forward line and the three-bar reversals plotted on the price chart and the DMI and the ADX plotted in separate sections below. Figure 9.3 displays my normal chart configuration. This chart is all I need to make decisions on whether to buy, sell short, or close a position.

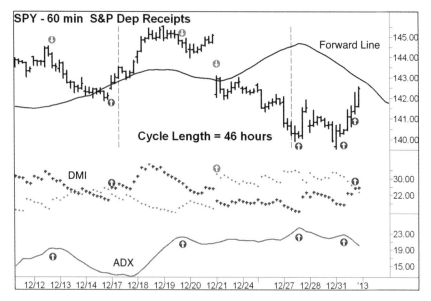

Figure 9.3 Standard chart depiction of favorite indicators in a stock price chart.

If I have a position, long or short, the first indicator I look at is the ADX. An ADX peak will immediately tell me when to close that position. It may not be a perfect indicator of the trend completion, but it is accurate enough for me to pay attention. I have found out the hard way that by not closing a position when an ADX peak occurred, I lost money. That is incentive enough to obey an ADX peak signal.

If I have a position and the ADX forms a trough, I will add to the position because an ADX trough signals that the existing trend is accelerating. It is also indicating that I now have a reliable closing signal. By rising, the ADX must peak at some time and tell me that the trend is over. An ADX low is, thus, a wonderful event because it not only makes money, but it also guarantees that I will have a reliable closing signal at or close to the end of the trend.

If I do not have a position in the stock, I still look at the ADX first to see if a peak has occurred in the recent past. Although an ADX peak by itself is a reliable signal for the end of a trend, it is not a reliable signal of a new trend. Further evidence is needed before I can enter a position. However, an ADX peak in a stock raises the possibility of a trend reversal (or in rarer instances, a continuation of the old trend) and, thus, is the first signal of change in the stock's behavior. From then on, I look for evidence supporting the beginning of a new trend in either direction.

New trend signals come from the price crossing the forward line, a DMI crossover, or the penetration of a three-bar reversal. Often, you will see both crossings at the same time along with a three-bar reversal breakout. This is the ideal time to initiate a position. The risks are small because the majority of evidence is favorable for a profitable trade. With such positive evidence, any subsequent adverse price move is unusual and, thus, a sign that something is wrong. When something is wrong, I want to return to cash and wait for additional evidence.

How many favorable signals do I require for an entry? Usually two, at least, and one of them must be *price*. The DMI and ADX are price related because they are indicators and derivatives of price behavior but are not prices themselves. A breakout through a three-bar reversal or a forward line, however, is direct price action. One or more of these must accompany the other signals.

Sometimes, I will take a "flyer" and act on skimpy evidence such as an ADX peak followed by a three-bar breakout. This kind of signal will usually occur long before a forward line breakout or a DMI crossover, and thus I will not enter a full position. Should the price later break the forward line or the DMI crossover, I will add to the position.

The DMI and forward line sometimes show what I call *equilibrium*. This is when the buying and selling pressure in the DMI are at roughly the same level and likely to cross in either direction. The stock's price may also be close to its forward line and could break in either direction. This equilibrium is often a period of low volatility in the stock. Low volatility always turns into high volatility when the stock price begins to move in a trend, but at this stage, it is impossible to tell the direction of any new trend. To take advantage of a new trend that I know will develop, but without knowing the direction, I wait for an actual crossover signal either in the DMI or through the forward line. I then place a "straddle" set of entry orders around the price bar that caused the signal. The majority of the time the new trend will be in the direction of the signal, but to be safe I place a buy stop with a fudge factor, a small fraction of the price, above the high and a sell stop with a fudge factor below the low of that bar. This set of orders will trigger if the break is legitimate and will automatically have a protective stop in place in the opposite direction in case the entry is a mistake. If the signal is false, chances are that the trend will resume in its old direction and trigger the other stop, again leaving the first untouched stop as protection in case there is a double reversal. If both the DMI and forward line crossing signals occur, I take a full position because this passes the requirement of a minimum of two signals. When only one signal occurs, I place an order for a smaller position. It can be increased later if the price behaves as expected.

Another factor to consider is price cycles alone. If the analysis of cycle period is successful, I can estimate when the next cycle low will likely occur. If I have a long position, for example, and the price is correcting into that expected low and is very close to it in terms of time but is still above its forward line, I know that the expected low will occur in the vicinity of the forward line, and I can thus place an entry order at that forward line level with minimal risk of loss.

Stops

The recent sudden "flash" crashes in the stock market make placing conventional protective and trailing stops hazardous. The sudden sharp declines (they always seem to be declines) can trigger stop orders prematurely. I use stops but carefully and only after they have been tested for robustness. I use a percentage and carry that percentage with the subsequent price action of the stock. For example, assuming a 2% risk, when I buy a position, I place a stop 2% below the entry price, and as the stock rises in price, I adjust the stop upward by the same percent measured from the highest price reached while the position is active. Thus, the percent stop becomes a trailing stop after the initial price rise. As an alternative, I also adjust the percentage for the trailing stop if the combined protective and trailing percentage produces poor results.

I always use an *entry stop* order when I see an opportunity. Too many times, an opportunity has turned out to be a false signal. To lessen that danger, I place an entry stop order slightly above or below the signal bar high or low on the day (or hour if I am trading shorter periods) following the signal. For example, if the signal is bullish, I determine the high of the price bar that caused the signal and add a fudge factor, something I have tested earlier, to that high for a buy stop order beginning the next day. Say the bar high was 23.5 and my usual fudge factor is 0.5. I would place a buy stop order for the next day at 24.0, which, if triggered, buys the position. If the signal was false, the stop order is not executed, and I'm clear and haven't been bagged.

Because it sometimes takes a day or two for the momentum to catch up with the signal, I usually keep the buy stop order active until it is obvious that the signal was false. On the other hand, when I receive a signal to close a position, I do it right away. There is no point in holding a dangerous position for any length of time because time works against any trade. I could have the money elsewhere in a less dangerous position and if none exist, cash is the best option. Those who don't act immediately on a closing signal are acting on hope that the indicator will change back to its earlier favorable reading. That is called "trading on hope," and it almost never works.

Experiments

Although I use the visual method of inspecting charts and their respective indicators for short-term, day-to-day trading, for this book I run several walk-forward optimizations on hourly price data to show that the method can be turned into an algorithmic trading system. To demonstrate that a combination of the indicators from Chapters 7 and 8 have value in trading, I perform a walk-forward optimization and analysis on the hourly data for the SSO (ProShares Ultra S&P 500) over the 600 trading hours from September 13, 2010 through December 31, 2012. It is limited to hourly data but could easily be adjusted for any bar period. I warn that these optimizations are for this book only and must be updated in the future if you choose to follow similar methods. You will also note that the parameters for the trading model end up differently than the ones I mentioned earlier in the cycle analysis. Those mentioned earlier reflect the assumption of cyclicality in stock prices. These optimizations disregard any theory of harmonics and look only at those parameters that produce robust results in out-of-sample data. The beauty of using this method in this case is that it needs no theoretical hypotheses other than those technical indicators applied in an algorithm.

The indicators I use in the optimization are the ADX peak, the ADX trough, and the forward line. The setup signals are triggered when any of the above indicators gives a signal, and entries are made when the price breaks a subsequent three-bar reversal. These are entry strategies. The exit strategies are protective and trailing stops of the same percentage. The point in this demonstration is to show that

ADX peaks and troughs and forward lines have predictive value in trading. In these demonstrations, I use hourly data but the principles are the same for any bar period. Optimizing of the variables is necessary, of course, and I advise not using the variables in this chapter because they are likely out of date by the time you are reading this. However, I trust that the demonstrations using simple entry and exit strategies are clear and show how well these principles work.

Table 9.1 shows the primary results of a walk-forward optimization of hourly data over 600 trading days in the SSO using different trading criteria. You will notice that the optimized parameters imply a different cyclicality to each security than what would be expected from classic cycle analysis and from the expectation for stock market indexes to have similar cyclical properties. The reason for this disparity is not that classical cycle analysis is wrong but that optimization has improved upon it by discovering the ideal lengths for each of the indicators. The use of classical cycle analysis is still valid and should be used when just eyeballing charts for trade setups. The optimized parameter results should be used when software is available to take advantage of more precise calculations and when the security under analysis has a performance history that lends itself to such methods. The ADX and the forward line are not applicable to many securities and should not be automatically presumed as valid. Only testing for results will assure that they can be used in the security of interest.

Table 9.1 Walk-Forward Analysis of ADX Peaks, ADX Troughs, and Forward Line Crossovers in the SSO (ProShares Ultra S&P 500) Hourly Data Over 600 Trading Days from September 13, 2010, to December 31, 2012

	ADX Peak	ADX Trough	Forward Line
Runs	15	10	20
OOS%	10%	15%	10%
FWL Length		14	12
ADX Length	6	78	
Bar Count	3	2	3

	ADX Peak	ADX Trough	Forward Line	
ADX Fudge Pct	0	5		
Sig Fudge Pct	0	1		
LX Prot Pct	3	13	3.5	
SX Prot Pct	2	6	1.5	
LX Trail Pct	10	13	9	
SX Trail Pct	7	6	4.5	
Initial Capital	$10,000	$10,000	$10,000	
OOS Ann NP$	$3,475	$5,593	$7,256	
OOS %Runs Prftbl	73.3%	90.0%	90.0%	s/b > 50%
OOS WFE	67.7%	54.9%	86.9%	s/b > 50%
# Calendar Days	796	798	798	
# Trades	73	58	149	
Avg Win/Loss	$2.72	$2.23	$2.02	
MDD%	1.31%	1.55%	1.42%	s/b < 20%
%Trades Prftbl	46.6%	60.3%	51.0%	s/b >50%
Avg Trade$	$126.73	$208.04	$86.54	
Profit Factor	2.37	3.39	2.11	s/b > 1.5
CAGR%	42.42%	55.19%	58.97%	s/b> 20%
MAR	32.38	35.61	41.53	s/b> 1.0
CPC	3.00	4.56	2.17	s/b> 2.0

Legend

Runs = Number of separate optimization runs within the data

OOS% = Percentage of each run data saved for out-of-sample test

FWL Length = Forward line length in hours

ADX Length = ADX length in hours

Bar Count = Number of bars in reversal pattern

ADX Fudge Pct = Amount by which ADX must reverse to signal

Sig Fudge Pct = Amount by which price must move beyond a three-bar reversal for signal entry

LX Prot Pct = Percentage protective stop below long entry

SX Prot Pct = Percentage protective stop above short entry

LX Trail Pct = Percentage trailing stop from long position high price

SX Trail Pct = Percentage trailing stop from short position low price

Initial Capital = $10,000 in all systems

OOS Ann NP$ = Out-of-sample annual net profit

OOS %Runs Prftbl = Out-of-sample percent of optimization runs that are profitable

OOS WFE = Ratio of out-of-sample annual profit to in-sample annual profit

Calendar Days = The number of days in the study from the first entry

Trades = The number of trades in the study

Avg Win/Loss = Gain for each dollar of loss

MDD% = Maximum drawdown percentage

%Trades Prftbl = Percent of all trades that are profitable

Avg Trade$ = Gain on average trade

Profit Factor = Gross profit divided by gross loss

CAGR% = Compound annual growth rate

MAR = Ratio of CAGR to MDD

CPC = Profit factor X avg win/loss X %trades profitable

Figure 9.4 shows the equity curve for the ADX peak signals in the SSO. Table 9.1 shows the pertinent statistical data from the walk-forward optimization and analysis. This system, like the others that follow, triggered only occasionally but still produced a compound annual percentage return of 43.6%. This system records when an ADX peaks and then signals when the price breaks either a three-bar reversal high or low. A break of the high indicates a buy and a break of the low indicates a sell. The tests showed that a fudge factor beyond the actual breakout price was unnecessary. The position close occurs when either a reverse signal occurs or when the position is stopped out either by the protective stop percentage or the trailing stop percentage. The maximum drawdown is relatively small at 1.31% and is the reason for the high MAR ratio. Each system described herein assumes a $.005 commission per share and a $0.10 slippage per share.

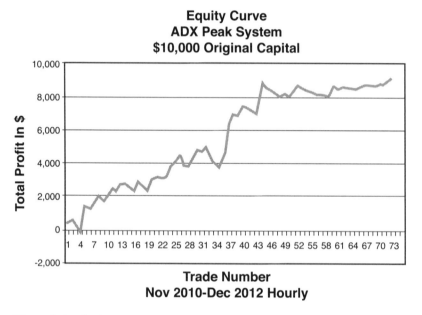

Figure 9.4 Equity curve of ADX peak signals in the SSO (ProShares Ultra S&P 500) hourly data over 600 trading days from September 13, 2010, to December 31, 2012.

The results from the walk-forward optimization and analysis of ADX troughs are demonstrated in the equity curve shown in Figure 9.5. This should be ample proof that the troughs in the ADX are as reliable as the ADX peaks for signals to act. The system is the same as for the ADX peaks, only the signals are qualified by being above or below the forward line. Only buy signals when the price was above the forward line were recorded and sell signals when the price was below the forward line. Otherwise the theoretical positions are closed either on the opposite signal or on a percentage stop. The compound annual return at 60.3% is considerably better than for the ADX peaks, and as the number of trades relative to the number in the other optimizations show in Table 9.1, the time in the market is relatively short. Indeed, by trading between ADX peaks and troughs, a trader can gain an even greater return because the signals obviously cannot occur at the same time but trigger independently. This allows a compound system to be developed that integrates both peak and trough ADX signals.

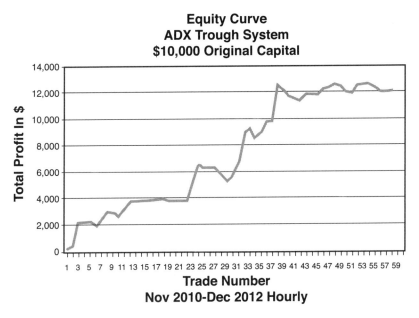

Figure 9.5   Equity curve of ADX trough signals in the SSO (ProShares Ultra S&P 500) hourly data over 600 trading days from September 13, 2010, to December 31, 2012.

Figure 9.6 shows the equity curve for the system derived from a simple crossing of the forward line with an upward cross a buy setup and a downward cross a sell setup. The action signals occur when the price breaks a three-bar reversal pattern. The results of this system show an even better return than the individual ADX systems with a 59.0% compound annual return.

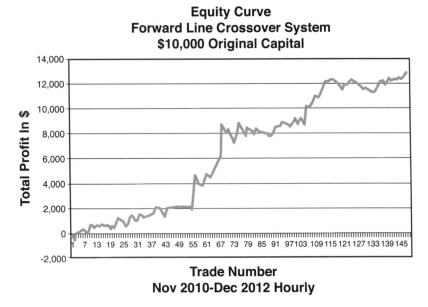

Figure 9.6 Equity curve of forward line crossover signals in the SSO (ProShares Ultra S&P 500) hourly data over 600 trading days from September 13, 2010, to December 31, 2012.

I hope you are now convinced about the merit of using the ADX peak and trough, irrespective of level, and the forward line as legitimate trading signals when integrated into systems using the three-bar reversal pattern. Variations of each and combinations of each are a starting point for the development of complex, robust trading systems. The studies show that the methods outlined in Chapters 7 through 9 have definite value and should provide the basis for many successful trading systems.

Conclusion

The unique technical methods described in Chapters 7 through 9, along with the discussion of how to combine them into a trading system in this chapter by thorough walk-forward optimization and analysis, show promise as profitable systems in the future. The theories behind each component indicator are realistically applied, and the results are without doubt encouraging. I use this general method on individual stocks with similar success and recommend that you consider this strategy as well. It seems to work for all time periods from hourly through weekly data and very likely in even shorter period data. It also works for any freely traded security, including commodities, financials, and other derivatives. The beauty of this system and the relative strength, stock selection, and investment system summarized in Chapter 5, "Stock Selection Using Relative Strength," is that they can be applied without expensive computer programming and with data and chart programs available for free on the Web. The stock selection system using the derived ratios for purchase and sale are good for many years to come, and the chart interpretation of the trading methods described in Chapters 7 through 9 are universal but could be improved upon with additional statistical study and development. They are applicable to anyone who has the time, energy, and inclination to pursue investment goals. You can be confident that these systems, when properly reoptimized and carefully applied, will profit in the future.

Index

Symbols

16-year cycles, 83-84
50-day average price, 47-48
50-day trading volume, 46

A

Abbott, G. C., 109
ADX (Average Directional Movement
  Index), 57, 91, 100-101
    analysis sequence, 132-134
    DX (directional index), 101
    how to use, 103-107
    peaks, 133
    plotting moving averages, 116-117
    rules for, 102-103
ADXR, 105
algorithmic investing versus
  discretionary investing, 1-3
amplitude, cycles, 112
analysis of cycles, 114-116
analysis sequence, 132-134
Ann NP$, 75
ATR (average true range), 91
    uses of, 94-95
    Wilder, Jr., J. Welles, 92-94
Average Directional Movement Index.
  See ADX (Average Directional
  Movement Index)
average true range (ATR), 91
    uses of, 94-95
    Wilder, Jr., J. Welles, 92-94

B

backtesting, 21-22
    entry strategies, 28
    equal-dollar weighted index, 31-33
    equity curve overfitting, 26-27
    equity curves, 24-27
    exit strategies, 28-31
    objective function, 33-34
    procedures, 35
    rules, relative strength, 22-23
    standard optimization, 22
    walk-forward optimizing, 24
beta, 14
Blumenthal, Earl, 109
Buffett, Warren, 2
business, investing, 6
buy rank, standard optimization,
  42-43
buy-and-hold system versus standard
  optimized system, 71

C

CAGR (compounded annual growth
  rate percentage), 18
%CAGR, 75
Capital Asset Pricing Model, 14
cash received from sold stocks, 72
Chartcraft, Inc., 73
Cohen, Abe, 109
commissions, 33
Commodity Systems Inc., 59

price data, 18
price targets, 16
  cycles, 116
prices, cycles, 110-111
procedures, 35
protective stops, 58
  walk-forward optimization, 67-68

Q-R

quarterly cycles, 111
ranking system, 70, 72
  walk-forward optimization, 74-77
raw system, walk-forward
  optimization, 77-80
relative price strength method, 10
relative price-to-sales ratio, 10
relative strength, 8, 69
  market timing, 80-81
  review and present standing, 69-71
  walk-forward optimizing
    ranking system, 74-77
    raw system, 77-80
Relative Strength Index, 91, 128
relative strength rules, 22-23
reversion-to-mean traders, 85-87
risk management. *See* exit strategies
robustness
  Value Line Geometric Index, 64-65
  walk-forward optimizing, 63
RSI (Relative Strength Index), 91, 128
R-squared, 76
rules
  for ADX and DIs, 102-103
  backtesting relative strength rules,
    22-23
  standard optimization, 22
%Runs Profitable, 76

S

S&P 500, 51
  market timing, 81
sample database size, standard
  optimization, 39

sell rank, standard optimization, 43
Sharpe ratio, 12-13, 76
shifts, cycles, 112
short trades, 88
slippage, 33
Soros, George, 2
standard optimization, 18-19, 37-38,
  60-61
  50-day average price, 47-48
  backtesting, 22
  buy rank, 42-43
  degrees of freedom, 38-39
  lookback, 40-42
  percent stops, 44-45
  rules, 22
  sample database size, 39
  sell rank, 43
  trading volume, 46
standard optimized system versus
  buy-and-hold system, 71
stops, 135-136
  protective stops, 58
    walk-forward optimizing, 67-68
straddles, 134
strategies, 7-8
  Capital Asset Pricing Model, 14
  entry strategies, 7-11
    backtesting, 28
  exit strategies, 7, 14-16
    backtesting, 28-31
  money management strategies, 16
  TradeStation method, 60
systems
  defined, 5
  O'Neil CANSLIM method, 5

T-V

testing, walk-forward optimization, 9
three-bar reversal, 130-131
TR (True Range), 92-93
Trades/Ann, 75
TradeStation method, 60
trading on hope, 136
trading strategies, 83-89

trading volume, standard
  optimization, 46
translation, cycles, 115
trend trading, 85
True Range (TR), 92-93
Turtle System, 95
Value Line Geometric Index, 52, 59
    robustness, 64-65
vertical shift, cycles, 112
volatility, 12-13, 88
Volatility Index, 91

W-Z

walk-forward optimization, 9, 17-19,
  59-67, 73
    backtesting, 24
    experiments, 136-142
    protective stops, 67-68
    ranking system, 74-77
    raw system, 77-80
    robustness, 63
WFE (walk-forward efficiency), 76-77
Wheelan, Alexander, 109
Wilder, Jr., J. Welles, 91
    ADX (Average Directional
      Movement Index), how to use,
      103-107
    ATR (average true range), 92-94
    moving averages, 92-94
    rules for ADX and DIs, 102-103

FINANCIAL TIMES

In an increasingly competitive world, it is quality
of thinking that gives an edge—an idea that opens new
doors, a technique that solves a problem, or an insight
that simply helps make sense of it all.

We work with leading authors in the various arenas
of business and finance to bring cutting-edge thinking
and best-learning practices to a global market.

It is our goal to create world-class print publications
and electronic products that give readers
knowledge and understanding that can then be
applied, whether studying or at work.

To find out more about our business
products, you can visit us at www.ftpress.com.